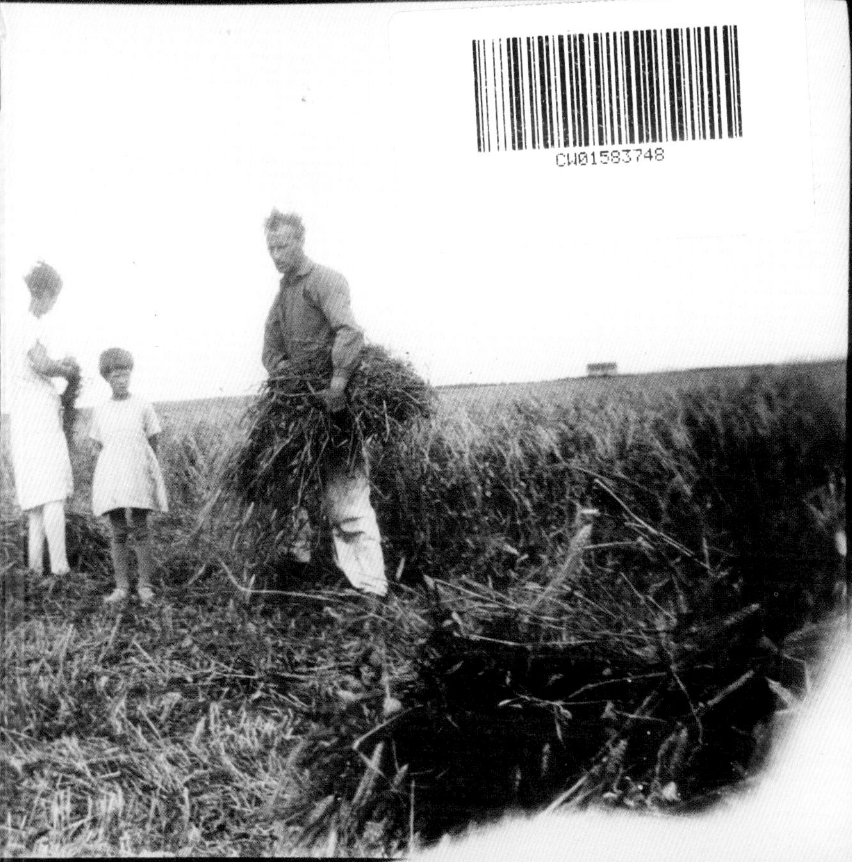

Art Souvenir – Hannah Ryggen – The Weaving Humanist

Series Editors: Bjorn Jonasson & Helgi Hilmarsson
Published 2019 by Gudrun Publishing, London

Artworks by Hannah Ryggen

English translation: Ingvild Andersen
Pictures on endpapers:
Unknown photographer/NTNU University Library

Project management: Bjorn Jonasson
Editorial assistance: Shauna Laurel Jones
Design: Helgi Hilmarsson

Printed in India

www.gudrunpublishing.com
www.artsouvenir.co.uk

ISBN 978-1-912366-10-1

art souvenir

Hannah Ryggen

The Weaving Humanist

Text by Solveig Lønmo

Gudrun

Table of Contents

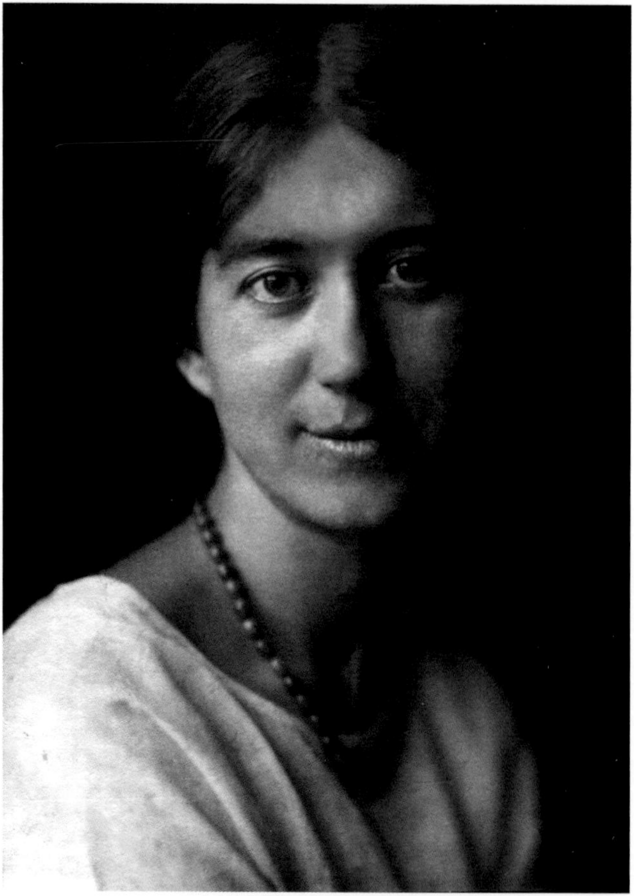

Hannah Ryggen, probably 1920s.

HANNAH RYGGEN
1894–1970

by Solveig Lønmo

I

Carefully, the monumental tapestry was brought out from underneath layers of dust, shards of broken glass and building debris. The artwork was located in the building that a few days earlier had been the target of a brutal act of terror. The screams had fallen silent, but the shock from the bomb explosion had not yet settled. The heavy tapestry was carried outside and transported away from the site.

Vi lever på en stjerne ("We Live upon a Star") (1958) is the title of the tapestry Hannah Ryggen created for the new government building in Oslo some 50 years earlier. She took the opportunity to weave a motif that would remind the politicians – every day as they entered the building to go to work – what it is their duty to protect in this world. *Vi lever på en stjerne* depicts our planet, inhabited by people who work and love, surrounded by outer space, stars and comets, giving the viewer a poetic reminder of how we should treat each other and the planet on which we live.

And now, in July 2011, the lower part of the tapestry had been torn, almost ripped apart. The tear was repaired by skilled conservators, who, despite mastering techniques that could hide the damage, opted to leave a visible scar. Thus, the event has become an integral part of the tapestry's story, symbolising the wound on our collective conscience. The contrast between Ryggen's message in *Vi lever på en stjerne* and the violence that was exerted is so vast – and looking back at Ryggen's oeuvre, it would be safe to assume she would have commented on the events of 22 July 2011 with a tapestry if she were still alive. And she would have shown the terrorist no mercy.

II

Hannah Ryggen fearlessly portrayed dictators and leaders of state, steeped in satire, from the 1930s until the 1960s, using tapestry as her chosen medium. Through her work she revolutionised the slow and traditionally decorative medium, turning it into an outlet for expression and scathing political critique. From her base at Ørlandet, a small, windy municipality at the farthest end of the Trondheim fjord, she would react instantly to world events by taking to her loom. Her disturbing piece *Drømmedød ("Death of Dreams")* (1936), a reaction to the burgeoning rise of Nazism, exemplifies how ahead of her times and foresighted she was. She would always weave as events unfolded, rather than in the safety of retrospect. Who was this formidable artist?

Hanna Jönsson was born into a working-class family in Malmö, Sweden, in 1894. She trained as a teacher, but never enjoyed this vocation. She was an avid reader and took classes in drawing and painting in her spare time. Her art tutor, Fredrik Krebs, encouraged her to go on a field trip to Dresden, Germany. She followed up on his advice in the summer of 1922, and this is where she met Norwegian painter Hans Ryggen, allegedly by mistake as she knocked on the wrong door.

During this time, as she entered a phase of artistic development, she realised she was not meant to express herself through painting, but through tapestries. The discipline would allow her to create art all the way from the raw materials to the final piece, a process she would eventually come to perfect, every step of the way. By choosing this alternative medium, she was also able to escape the tendency of the times to regard women's artworks as inferior compared to those of their male peers.[1]

Hannah moved to the Ryggen farmstead at Ørlandet for love. Everything the local landscape could offer became part of Hannah Ryggen's creative exploration. Natural resources such as lichen, bark and heather could be used for dyeing yarn, and as such the

1 Marit Paasche, *Hannah Ryggen. En fri* (Pax Forlag, Oslo, 2016), p. 29

tapestries are closely linked to the place she made increasingly her own. The animals at the farm provided them with food on the table and became essential parts of everyday life.

In fact, everyday life inspired some of her first large-scale tapestries. In works like *Vi og våre dyr ("We and Our Animals")* (1934), nature is not depicted as a romantic notion, but as an experience. Unlike the metropolitan experiences that were frequently depicted in European art at the time, the tapestry reveals a tough, sometimes scarce, life in the countryside. The artist confides in us details of her life, and the work is highly political in the sense that it tells a story about the conditions under which people must live their lives.[2]

When resources are scarce, one must use whatever means are available. How lucky, then, that urine provides the most glorious shades of blue! The lure of producing rich blue hues through this natural dyeing process led the artist to collect urine (preferably from males with a certain amount of alcohol in their system) in a

---

2 Paasche, *En fri*, p. 62 and p. 76

pot, mix it with indigo (as well as a secret ingredient), and let the sunlight heat it up to the right temperature. The wool yarn turns green when dipped into the mixture, but takes on a bold shade of blue after air drying.[3]

III

One recurring central motif of humanist Hannah Ryggen's tapestries is that of individuals who have suffered injustice. Via newspapers and the radio, the artist couple kept up to date on ever more shocking news from the mid-1930s onwards. Italy, led by Mussolini, invaded Ethiopia in 1935, despite the Italo-Ethiopian Treaty of 1928. Ryggen felt strongly provoked by this move, and she responded with the tapestry *Etiopia ("Ethiopia")* (1935). Emperor Haile Selassie is depicted dressed in beautiful garments and with a gentle face, whereas Mussolini has been decapitated, his head pierced by a spear. The monumental work, which only took a month of hard

3 Hannah Ryggen in a letter to her daughter Mona, May 1955

graft to complete, would become the first in a series of highly current tapestries. Alongside such works as Picasso's *Guernica* (1937), *Etiopia* was exhibited at the 1937 World Fair in Paris. Fearing diplomatic repercussions, however, its organisers tucked the part depicting Mussolini's chopped-off head away so it was hidden from view. The censorship only demonstrates the potential power inhabited by this artwork.

In 1936, the aforementioned *Drømmedød* became one of Ryggen's most significant works. The lower part of the grey and brown composition represents a brick wall, which, almost suddenly, appears to be a pattern of swastikas. The artist makes use of an existing language of symbols to create an optical effect, practically revealing how evil can exist underneath the decorative surface. In the top part, Carl von Ossietzky, the Nobel Peace Prize winner, can be seen, imprisoned and handcuffed. Three figures of evil,[4] their faces a dark red colour, strangle the "dreamer", whilst a figure who resem-

4 Joseph Goebbels, Hermann Göring and Adolf Hitler

bles Albert Einstein,[5] violin in hand, is able to make a break for it through the prison bars. Hannah Ryggen felt only art and science could save the world at this point. Armament for World War II was still on the increase, and even though Norway was not yet directly affected, this would not last.

One early morning in May 1944, the Nazis knocked on the door at the farm on Ørlandet. They barged in and inspected the artist couple's home, as they had caught wind of the Ryggens' political engagement. The Nazis suspected Hans Ryggen was expressing blunt resistance in his paintings, and they found what they were looking for. Hans was arrested. Hannah's rolled-up tapestries that laid on the floor, however, they did not bother to look at. They were, after all, just weavings made by some woman out in a marginal place in the provinces. If only they had known what the textiles were hiding.

The triptych *6. oktober 1942 ("6 October 1942")* (1943) represents Hannah Ryggen's reaction to a string of specific events that hap-

---

5 Ryggen may have seen a photograph of Albert Einstein with his violin, similar to the depiction in *Drømmedød*, in a Norwegian periodical in 1935.

pened during the war. The Nazis had an airport built at Ørlandet, exploiting prisoners of war to do the labour. On 6 October, the Nazis declared martial law in order to prevent further sabotage operations. In all, 34 Norwegian nationals were executed during martial law, which lasted for six days. Ryggen reacted with anger and a compulsion to comment through her art. Her monumental work includes the murder of theatre manager Henry Gleditsch. Behind the pietà-esque group of figures, in which Gleditsch falls into his wife's arms, a Serbian prisoner of war can be seen – he was allegedly tortured and killed over a negligible offence. Above them all, Hitler himself is seen hovering, wielding a gun in each hand. Hitler has been equipped with oak leaves protruding from his anus, a mocking inversion of a familiar symbol of strength and permanence often employed by the Nazis.[6] The mid-section of the tapestry depicts a gentle Winston Churchill in the Tower of

6 Steffen Wesselvold Holden, "Hannah Ryggen. Iconography and Activism", in *Hannah Ryggen. Weaving the World* (Nasjonalmuseet, Moderna Museet and Koenig Books London, 2015)

London, and the right section of the composition is dedicated to a family portrait. The Ryggen family dreamt of fleeing across the sea to England.

IV

After the war the family was able to visit Paris, which they had longed to do. The loom had to stay at home, but surrounded by museums and galleries, the artist could get a fresh breath of air and replenish creative inspiration. Ryggen started visualising future works in her mind, and over the years that followed she would realise them and exhibit widely both in Norway and abroad.

Ryggen was the first Norwegian textile artist whose work was acquired by the National Gallery in Oslo, and the first textile artist to exhibit at Høstutstillingen (the national annual autumn exhibition). She represented Norway in the 1957 Venice Biennale. Even though it would have made a significant difference to her private financial situation, she rarely sold her work to private buyers. Only in the public eye would the works be able to confront the viewer the way she intended. As Marit Paasche writes in her book *Hannah Ryggen. En fri* (2016), "Hannah Ryggen's tapestries say, 'This event has unfolded, and you need to be aware of it and take a stance.' Yet they are not merely illustrations, and they transcend the time and place in which they were created. The artworks are as valid now as they were then. They breathe."[7]

Hannah Ryggen's art is enjoying renewed interest today, nearly 50 years after her death. The tapestries are juxtaposed with contemporary international art by younger artists, and she gains ever more admirers. Unfortunately, Ryggen would still have had an abundance of events to react to in our current political climate. Who would she have chosen to portray in a satirical way today? Which situations would have led her to vent out anger and frustration in her tapestries? We can only assume she would have been just as sharp-witted; her art is exemplarily brave.

7 Paasche, *En fri*, p. 195

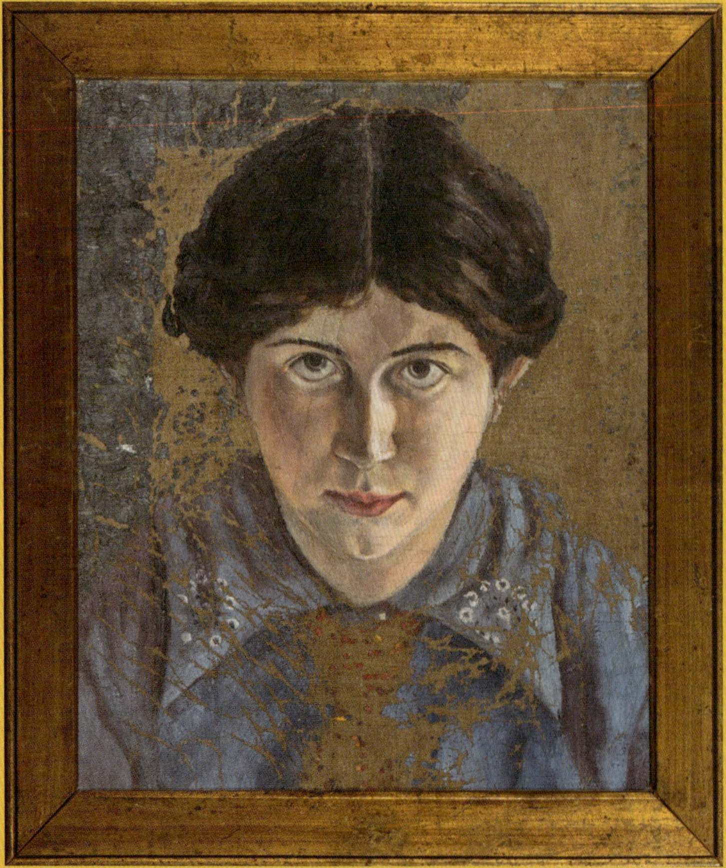

Self-portrait, 1914.
Oil on canvas.
40 x 33 cm

"Every man and every woman, wherever they may be on the social ladder, should be raised to know how to do two things: produce their own food and be self-sufficient. For anyone to be somebody else's servant is undignified. Everyone should work, nobody is above anyone else. Equal opportunities for all. We are all but flesh after all."

Letter from Hannah Ryggen to Andreas Schjoldager, 26 March 1942

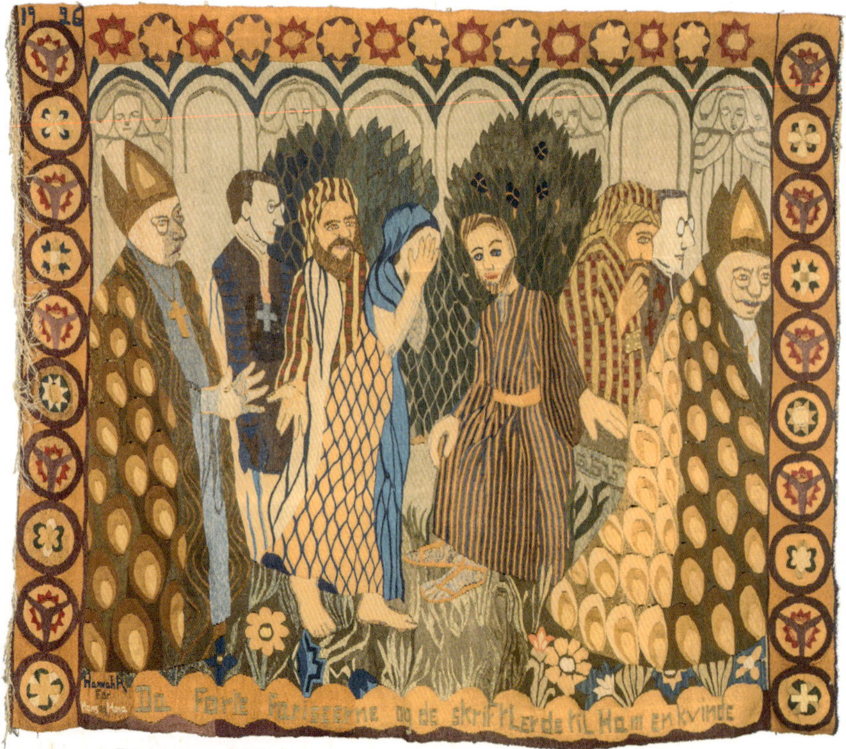

The Adulteress, 1926.
Tapestry in wool and linen. 190 x 222 cm

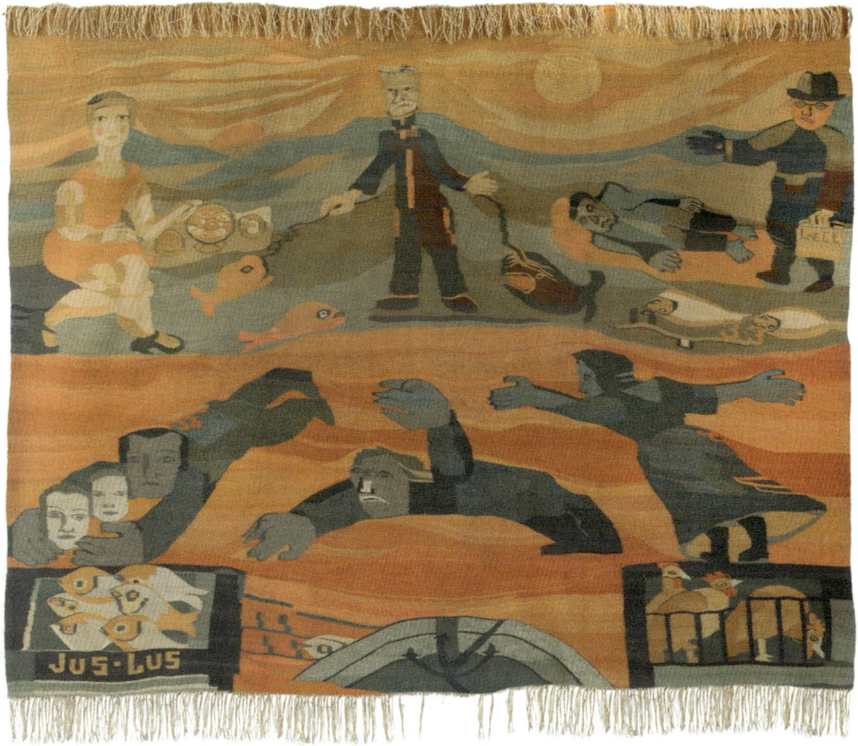

Fishing in the Sea of Debt, 1933.
Tapestry in wool and linen. 145 x 185 cm

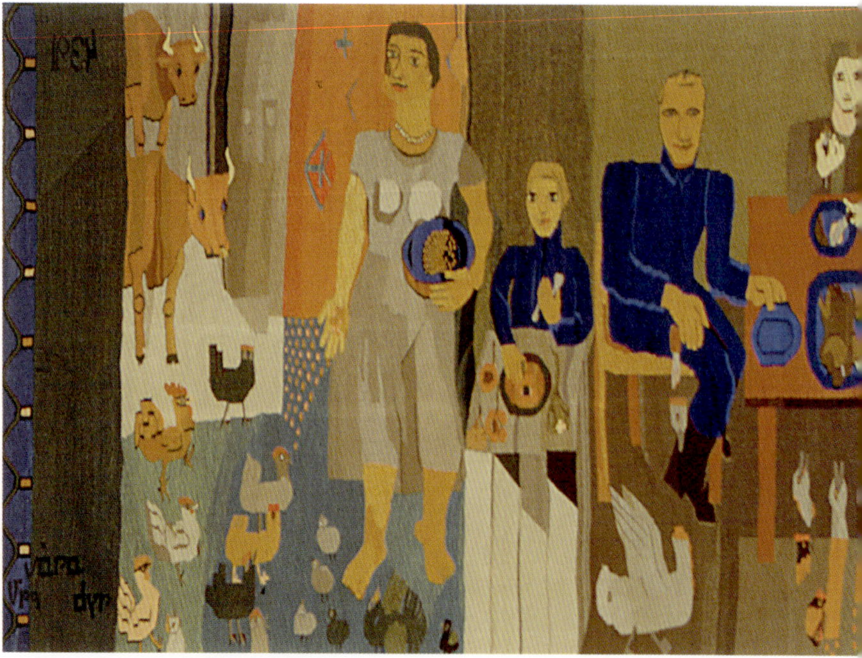

We and Our Animals, 1934.
Tapestry in wool and linen. 187.5 x 491 cm

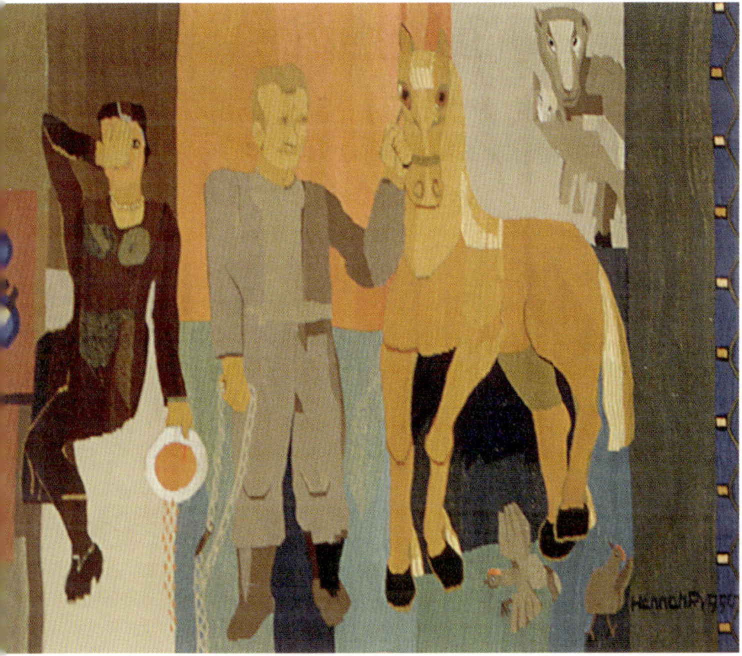

»
Death of Dreams, 1936.
Tapestry in wool and linen.
235 x 271 cm

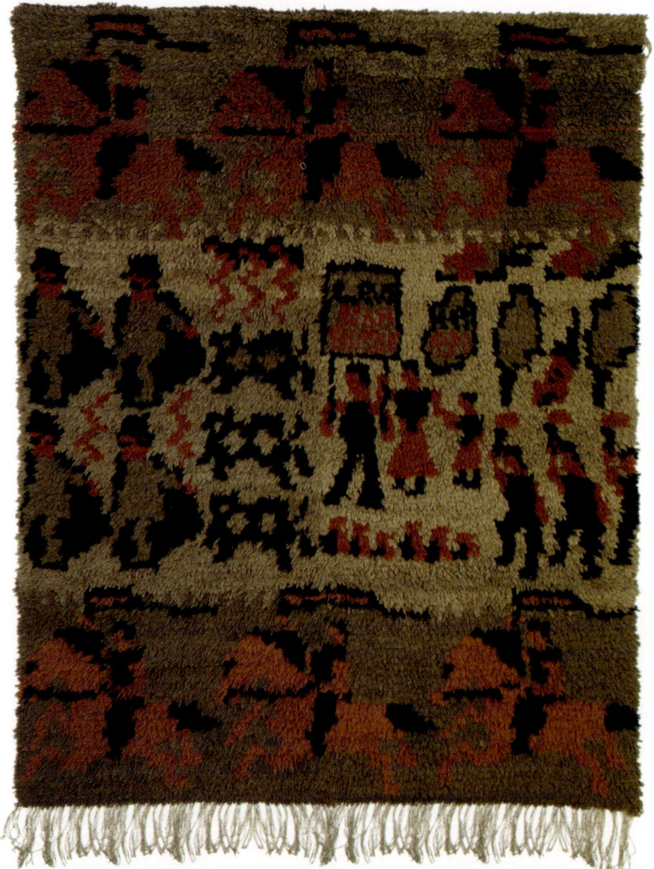

First of May Procession, 1935.
Rug in wool and linen. 172 x 140 cm

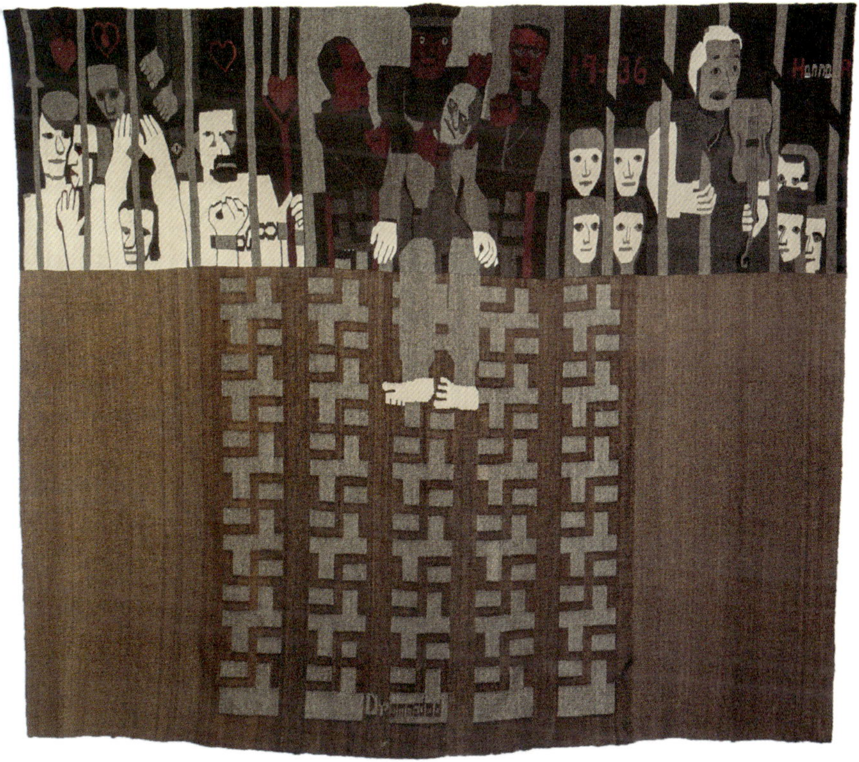

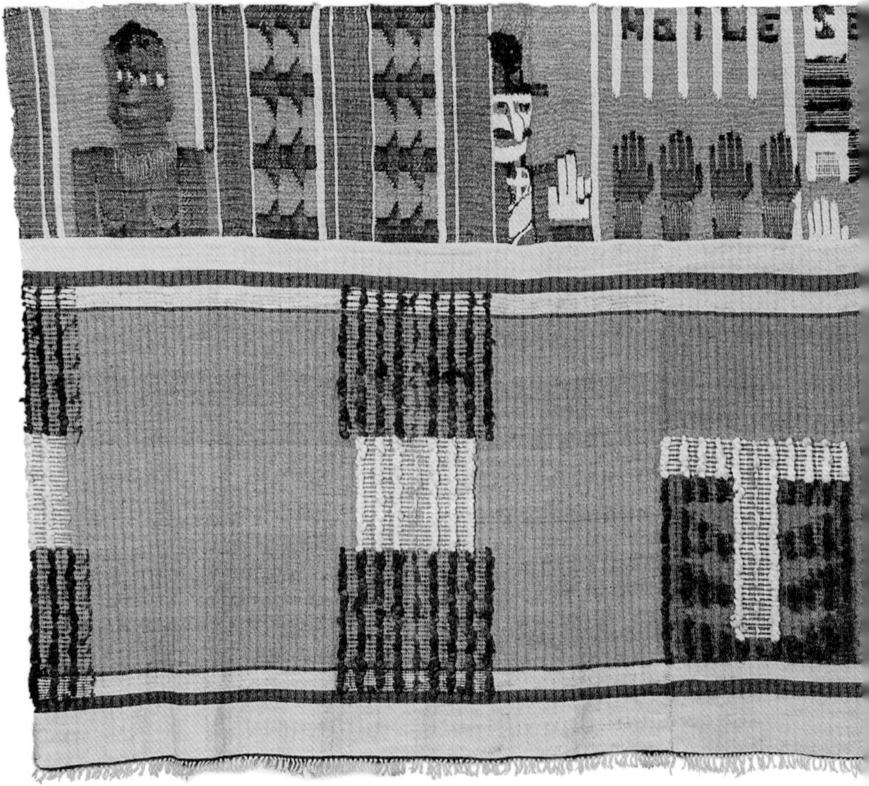

Ethiopia, 1935. Tapestry in wool and linen. 160 x 380 cm

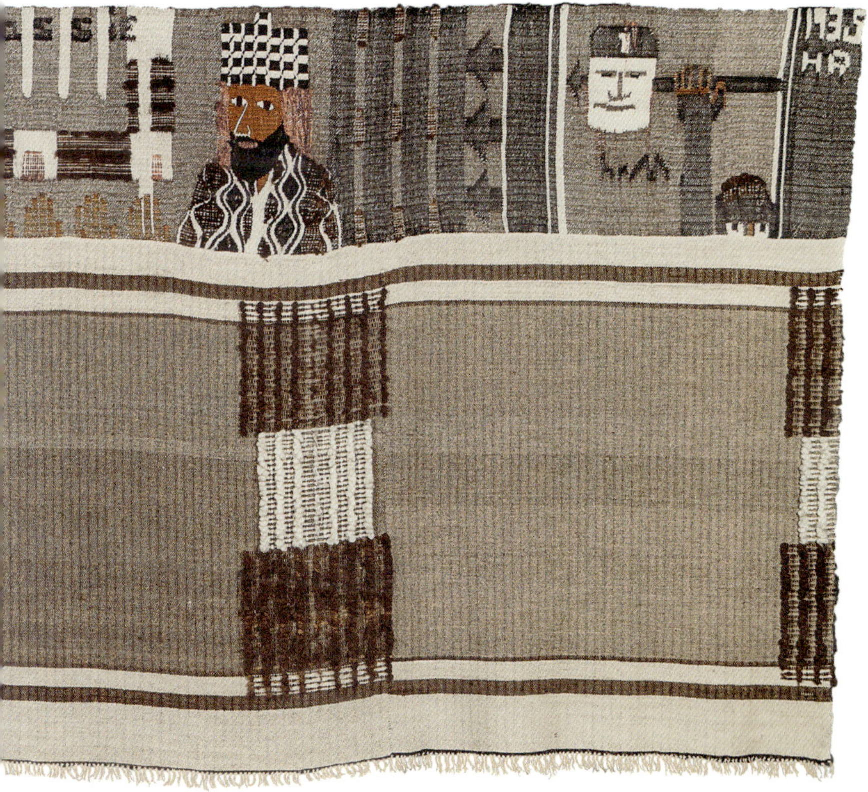

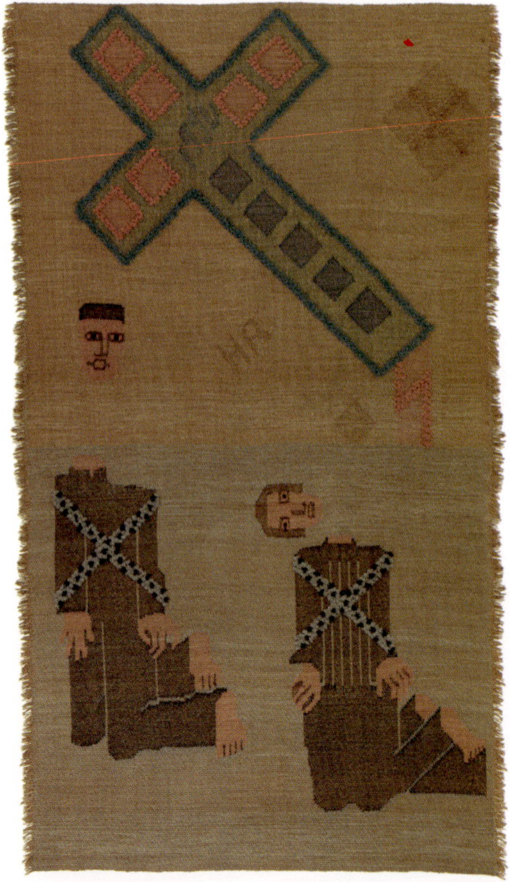

»

***Spain (La hora se aproxima)*, 1938.**
Tapestry in wool and linen. 193 x 219.5 cm

Daybreak, 1936.
Tapestry in wool and linen. 297 x 181 cm

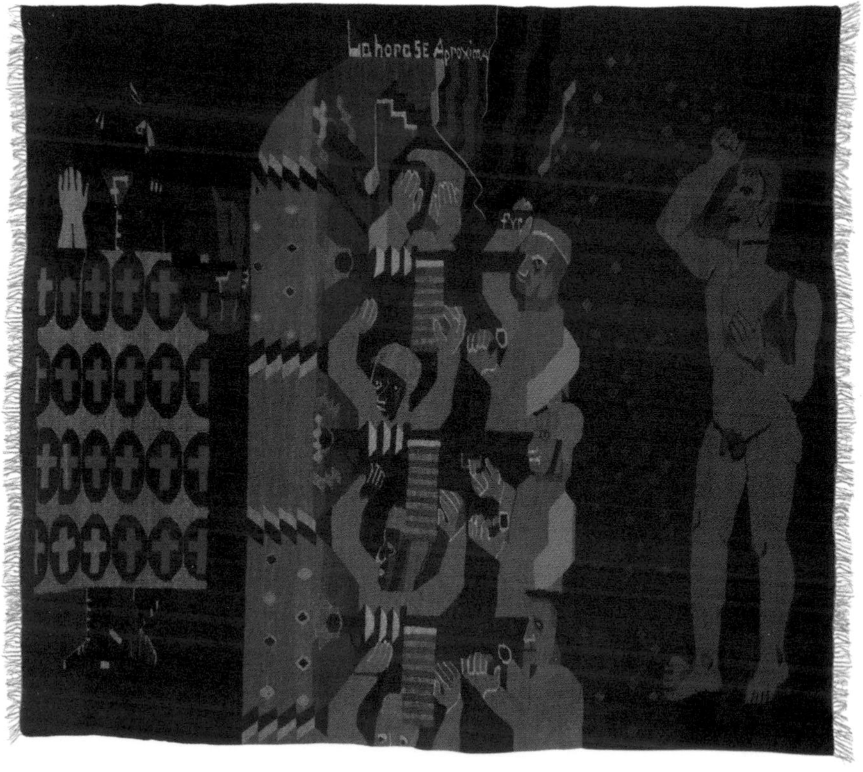
La hora SE Aproxima

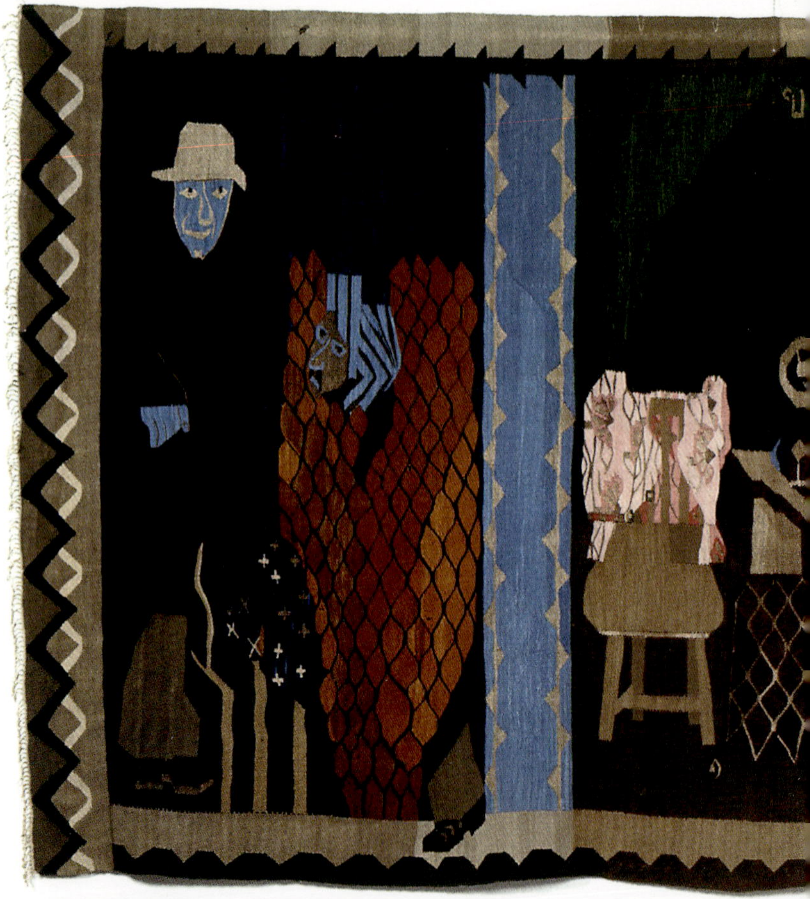

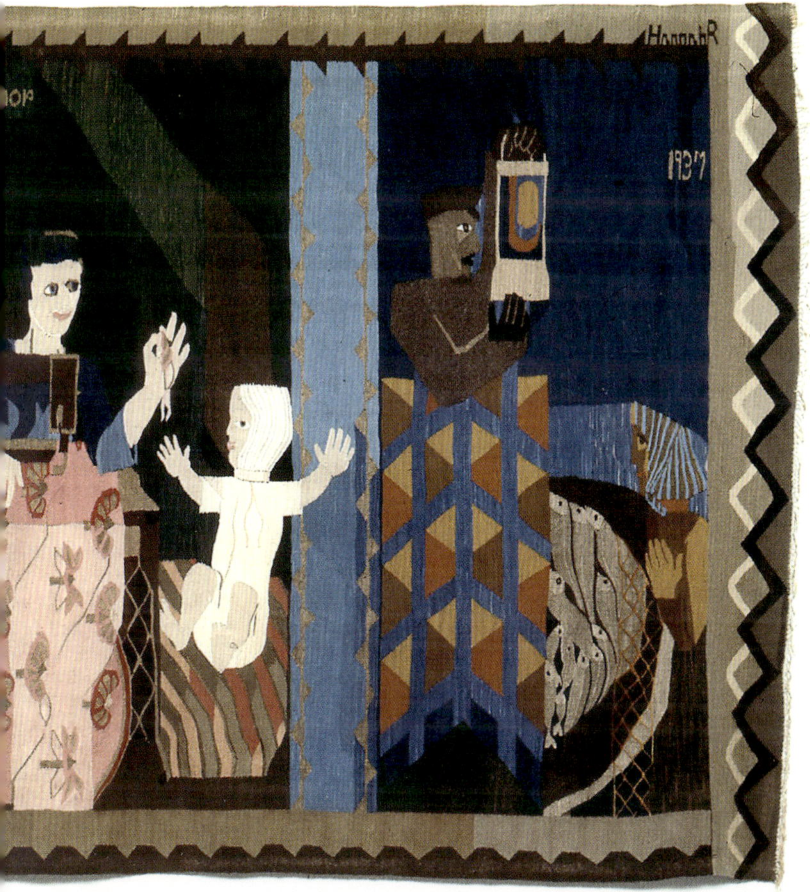

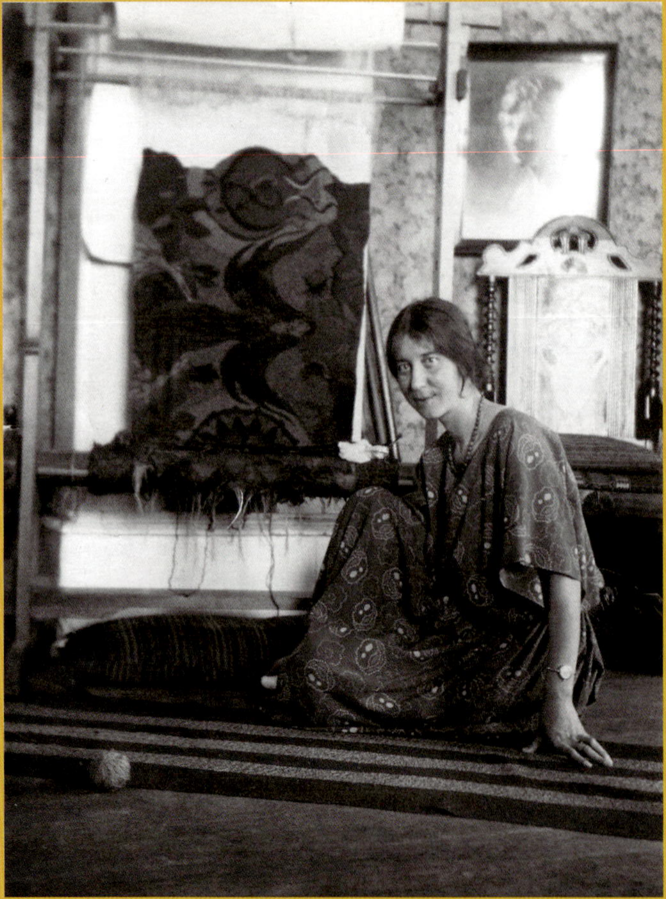

Pages 28–29
Unmarried Mother, 1937.
Tapestry in wool and linen.
185 x 385 cm

Hannah Jönsson, 1922.

"Like a painter in front of his empty canvas, I believe the weaver should sit in front of her loom, with no pattern, no other tools to aid her. Just like the painter uses his fantasy to create the painting on the canvas, I want the weaver to create the tapestry using her fantasy. Only then does weaving become an art form in its own right!"

Interview in local newspaper
Adresseavisen, *3 May 1930*

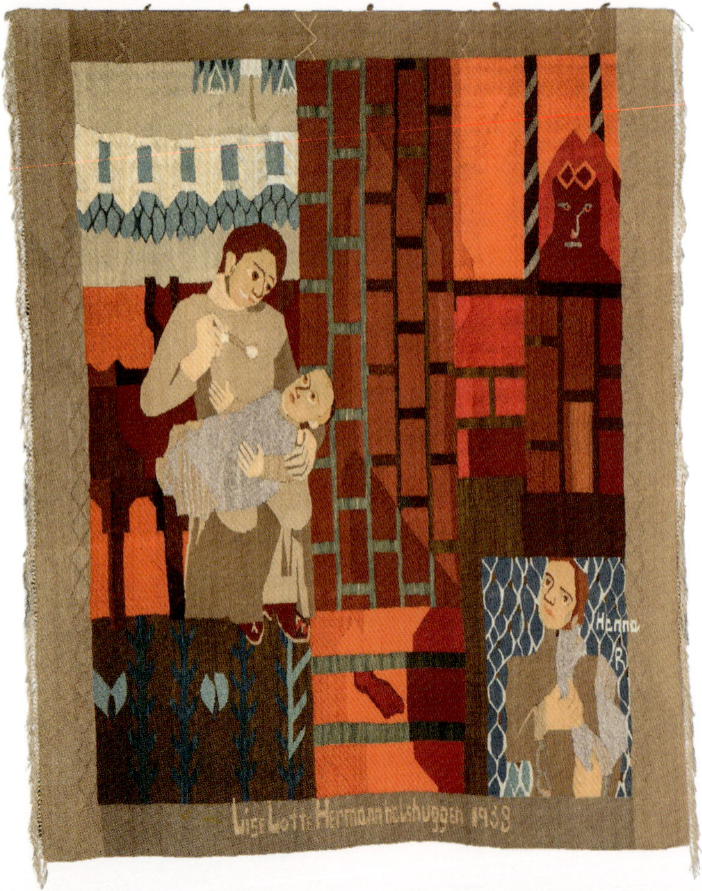

Liselotte Hermann decapitated, 1938.
Tapestry in wool and linen.
190 x 155 cm

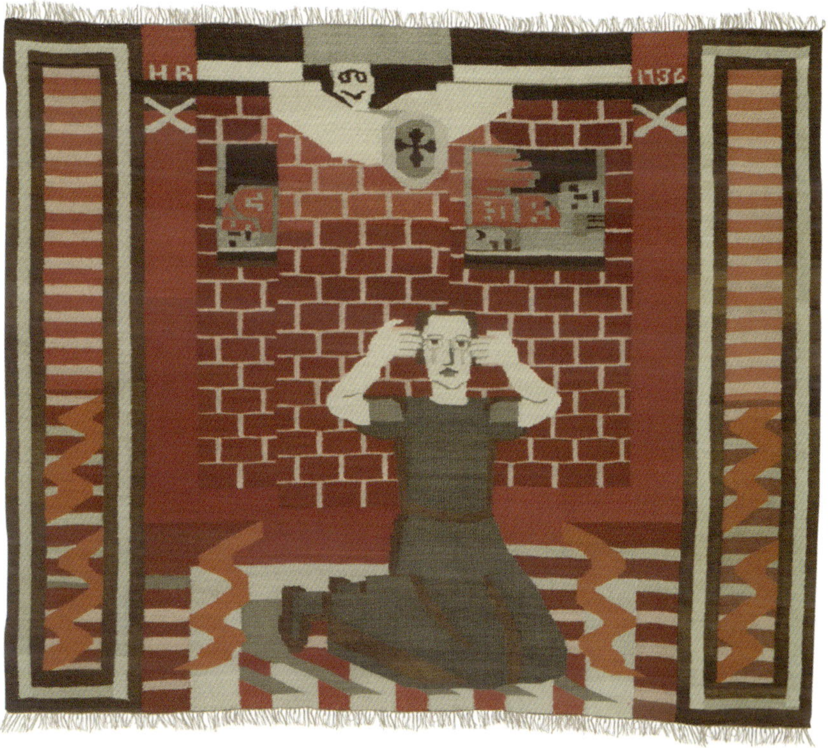

Horror, 1936.
Tapestry in wool and linen. 147 x 180 cm

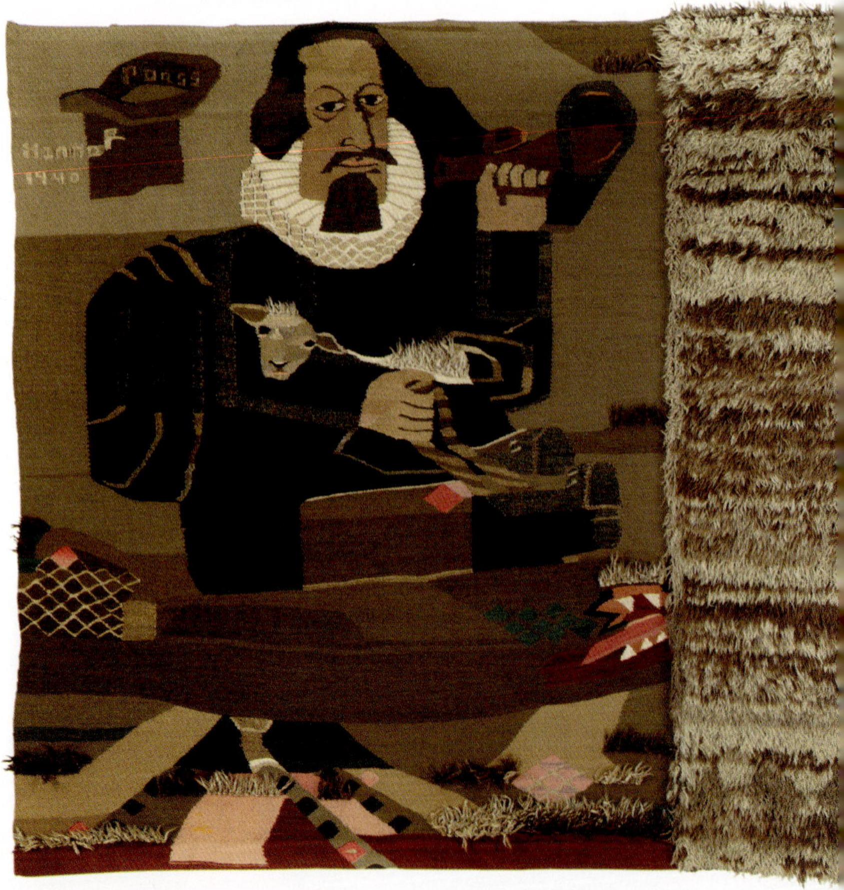
1940

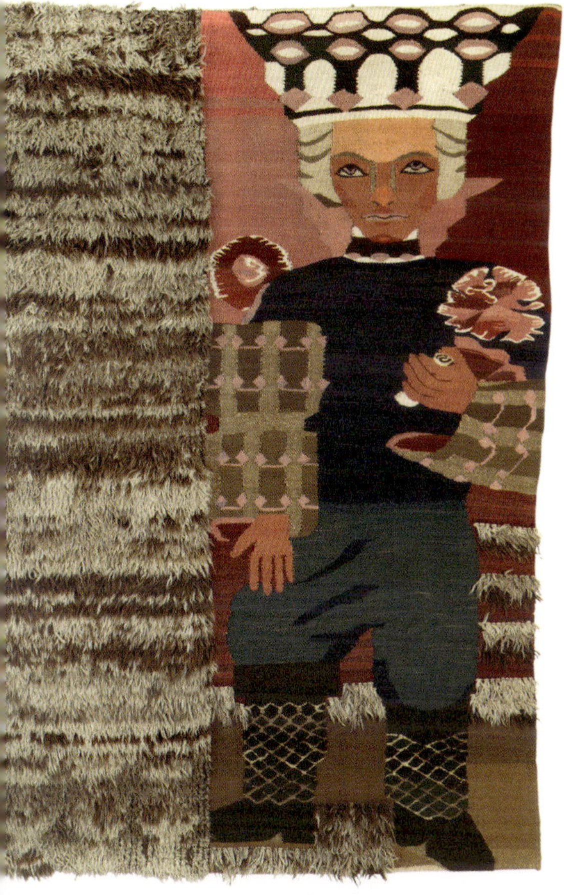

Petter Dass, 1940.
Tapestry with pile in
wool and linen, rug.
147 x 258.5 cm

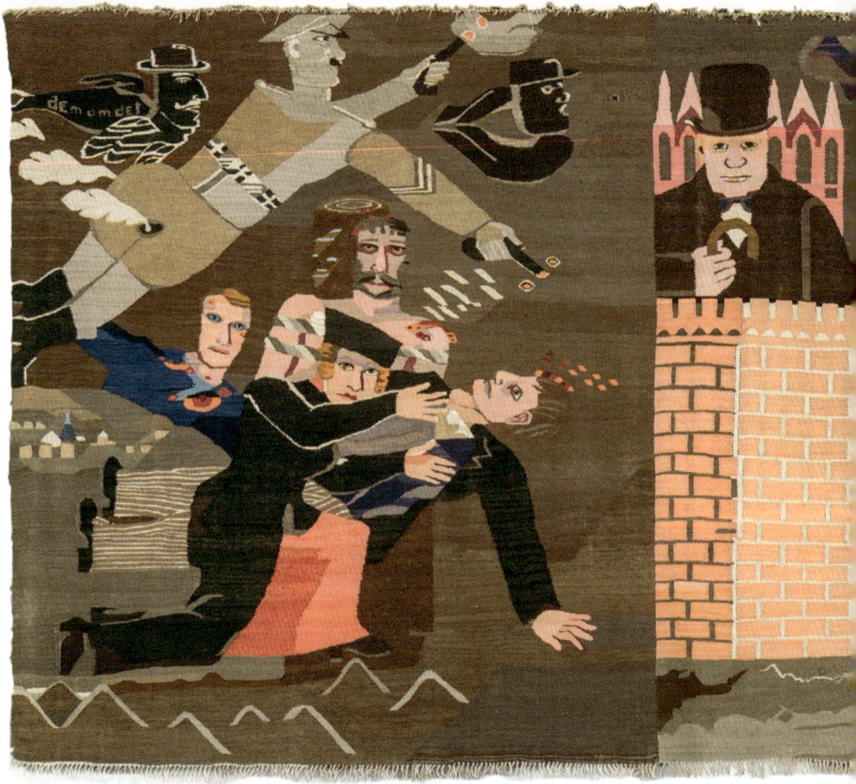

6 October 1942, 1943.
Tapestry in wool and linen. 170 x 420 cm

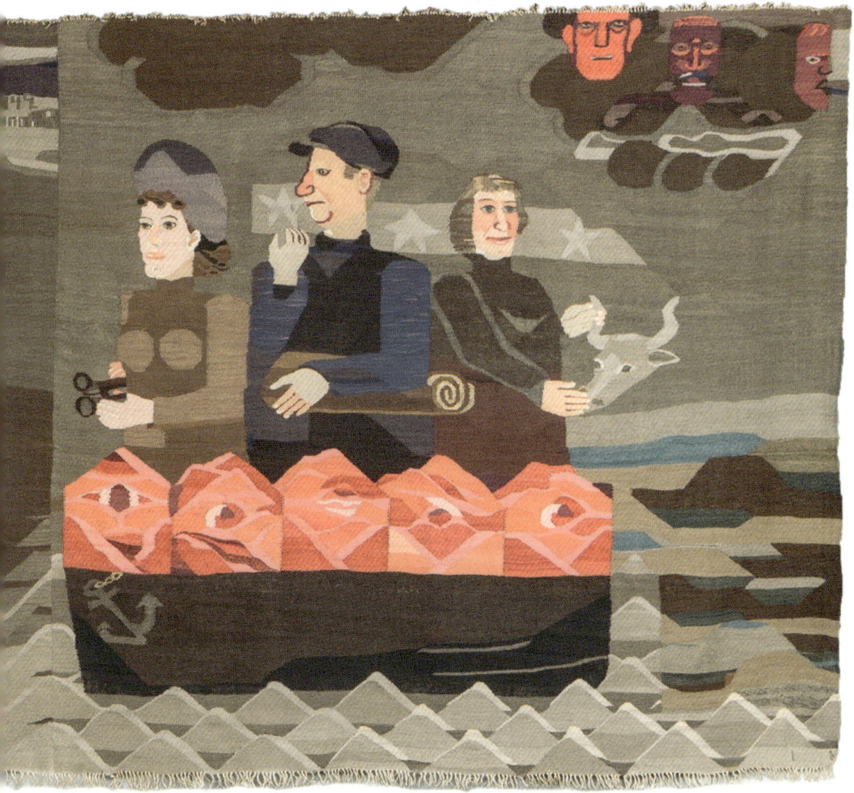

Page 40

The Prison Camp Grini, 1945.
Tapestry in wool and linen.
190 x 170 cm

Page 41

Mother's Heart, 1947.
Tapestry in wool and linen.
195 x 190 cm

Page 42

Schweden, 1946.
Tapestry in wool and linen.
190 x 175 cm

Page 43

A Free One, 1948.
Tapestry in wool and linen.
190 x 200 cm

Freiheit, 1941.
Tapestry in wool and linen. 190 x 193 cm

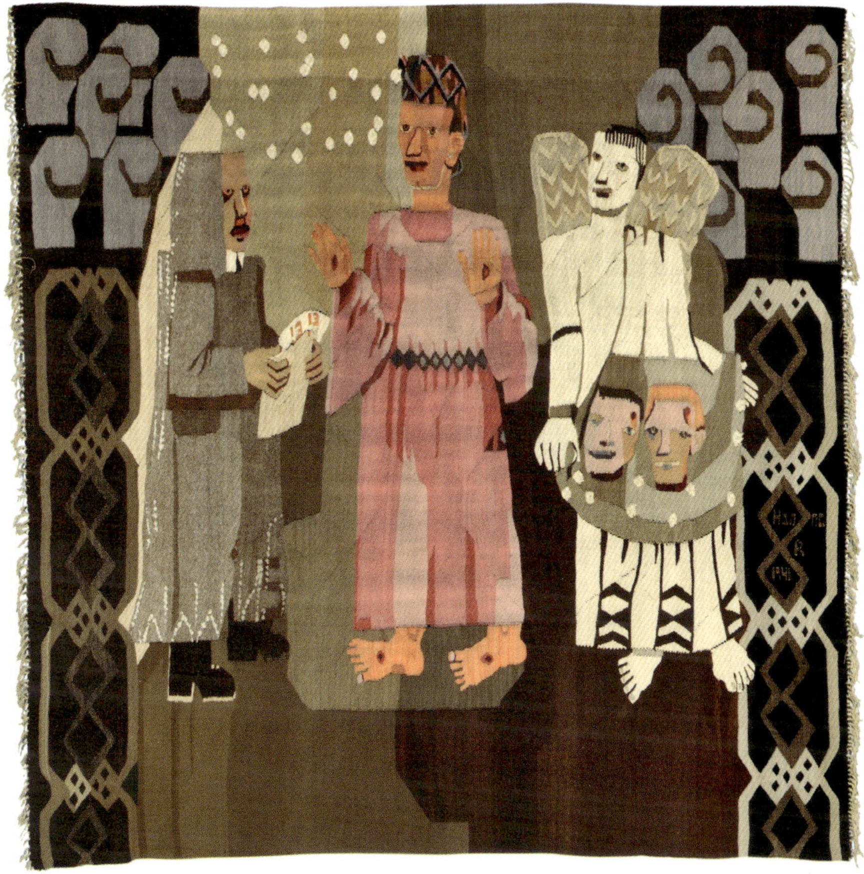

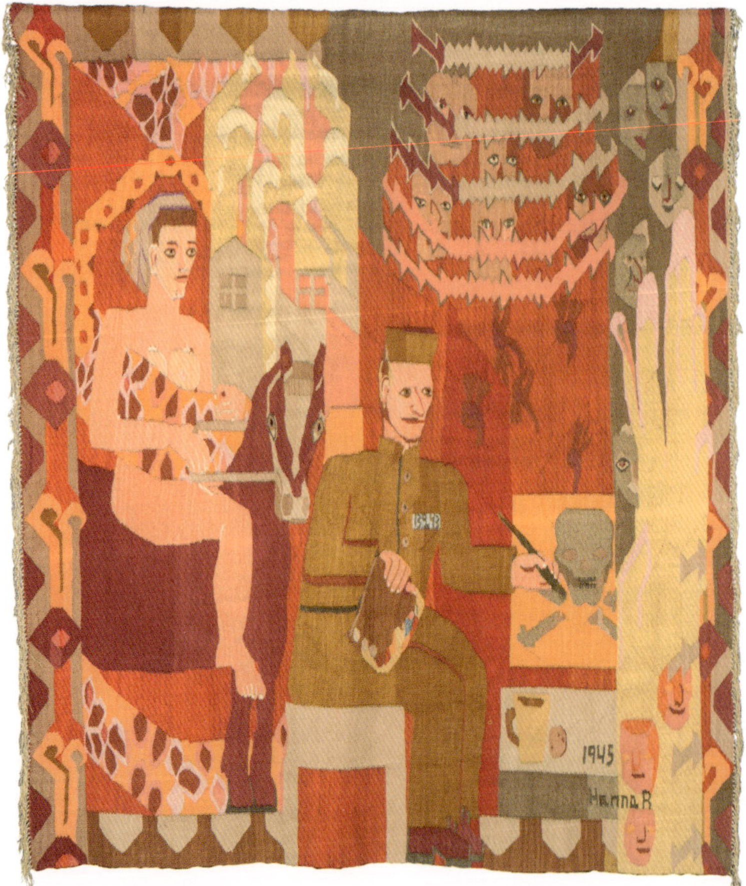
1945
Hanna R

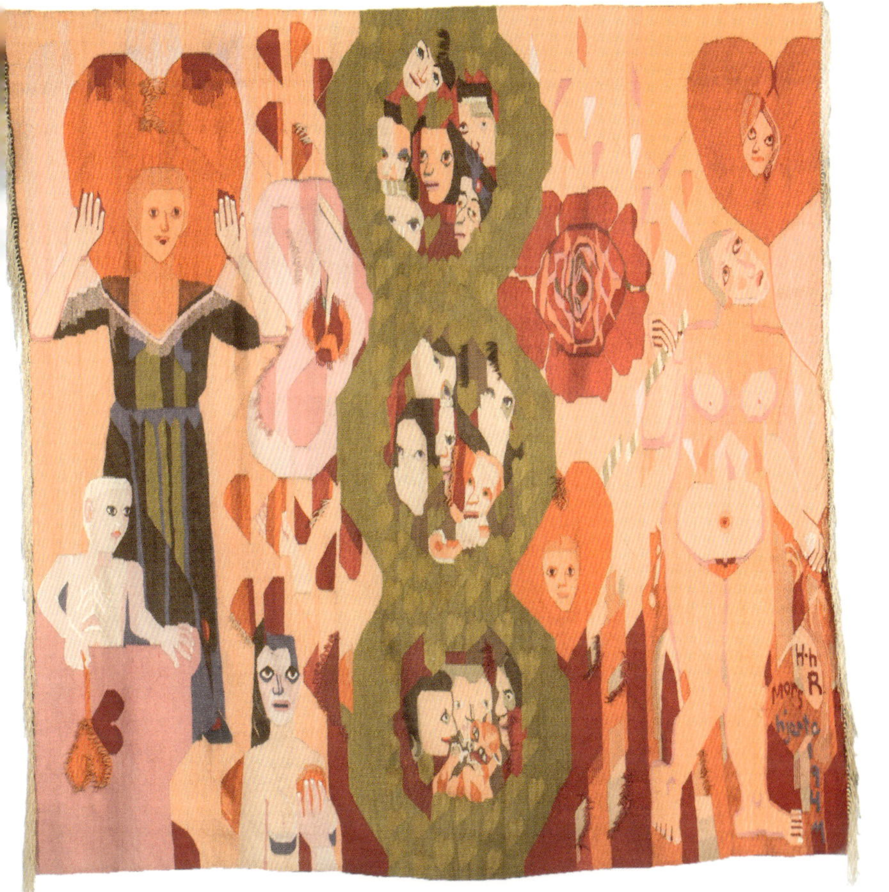
H·h
R
Mors

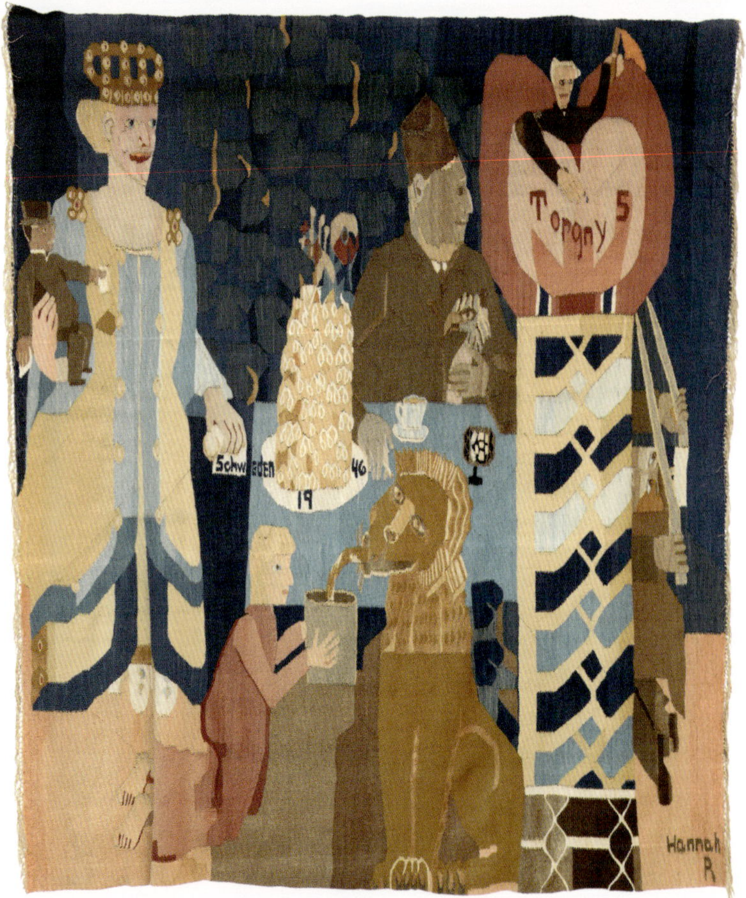
Torgny 5
Schweden 46
19
Hannah R

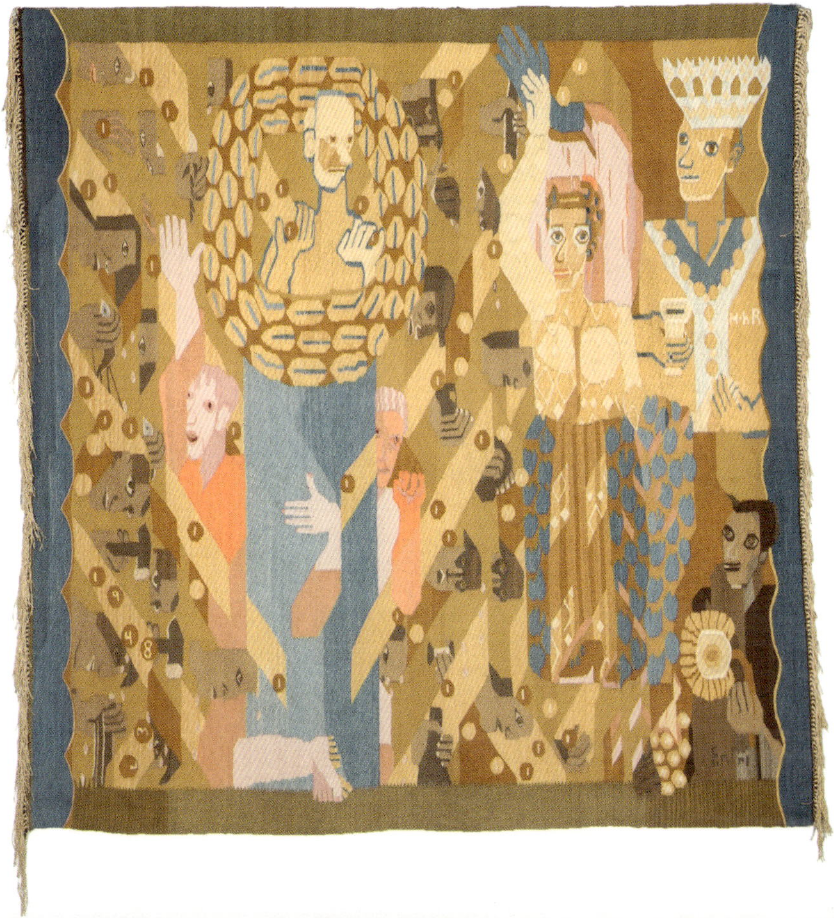

"This fills my life with purpose. I employ all my strength; spiritual as well as physical, in my work [...] it is like entering a fairy tale, and staying there until the work is finished. Then let others be the judge."

Interview in Swedish newspaper Arbetet, *May 1958*

Hannah Ryggen by her loom, date unknown.

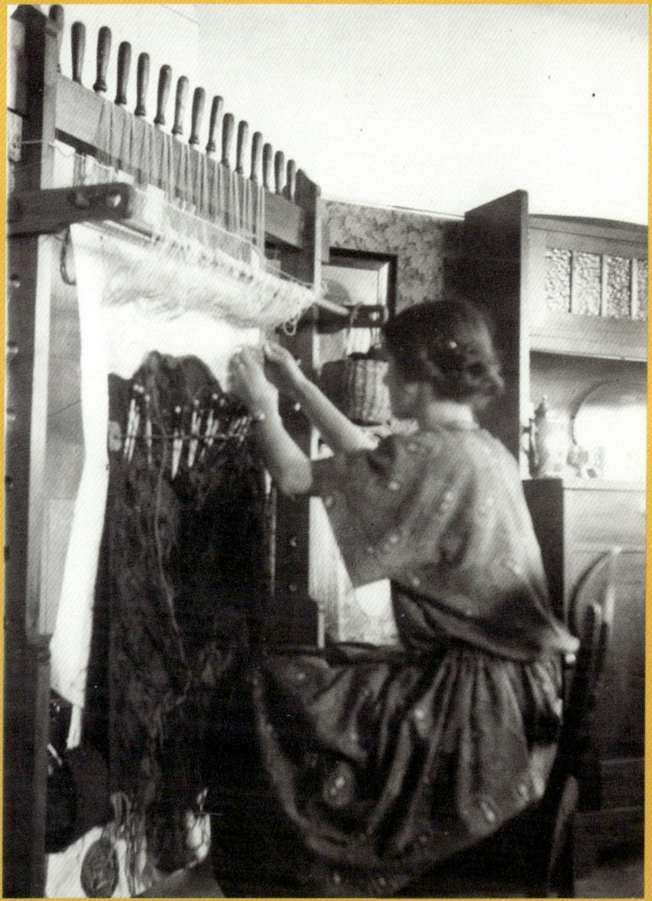

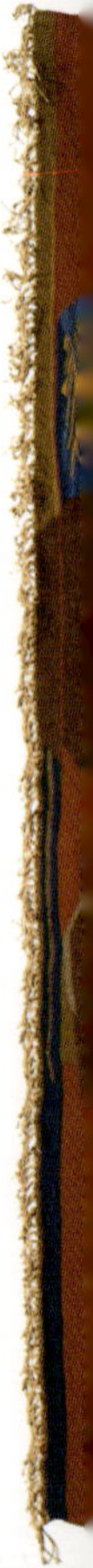

The Use of Hands, 1949.
Tapestry in wool and linen.
190 x 210 cm

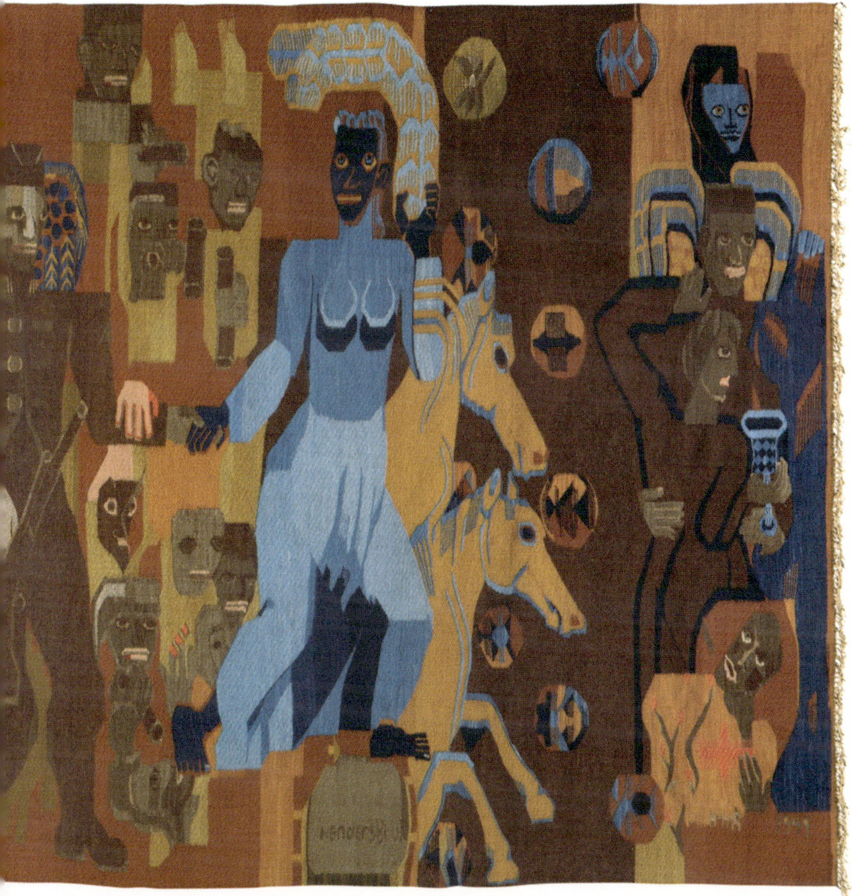

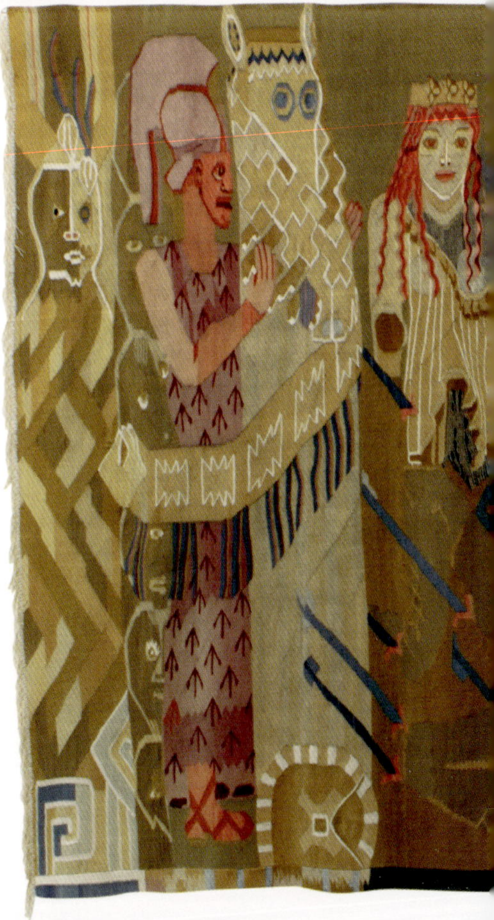

Trojan Horse/The Picasso Tapestry, 1949–58.
Tapestry in wool and linen.
190 x 320 cm

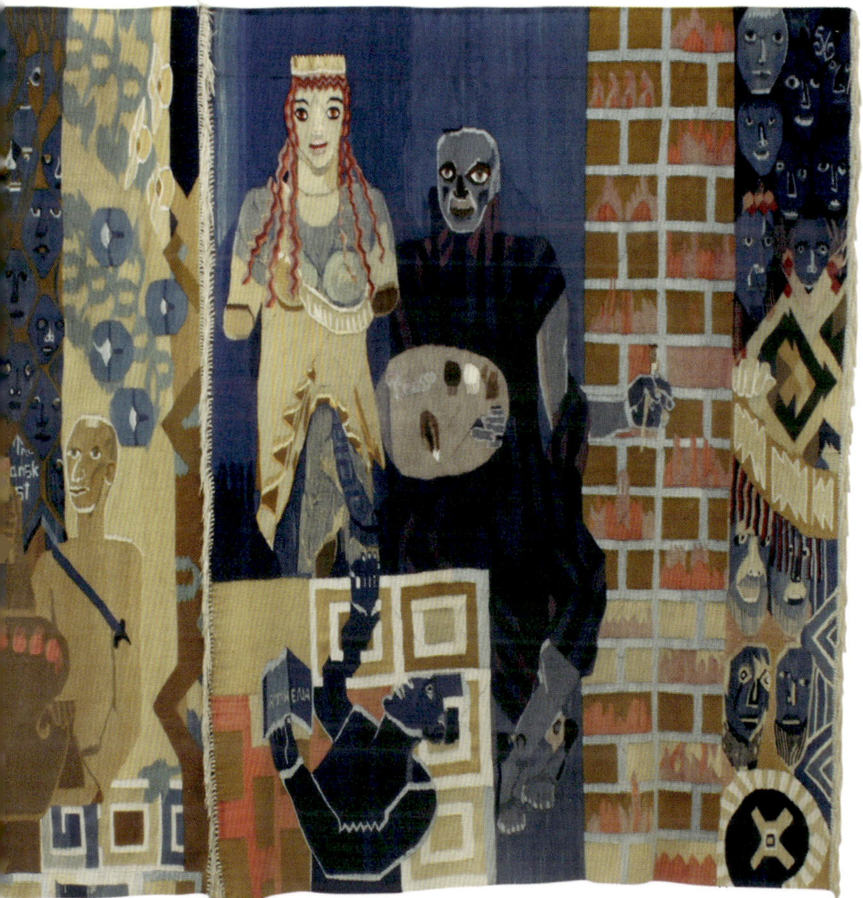

Ja, vi elsker (the title of the Norwegian national anthem), 1950.
Tapestry in wool and linen.
222 x 190 cm

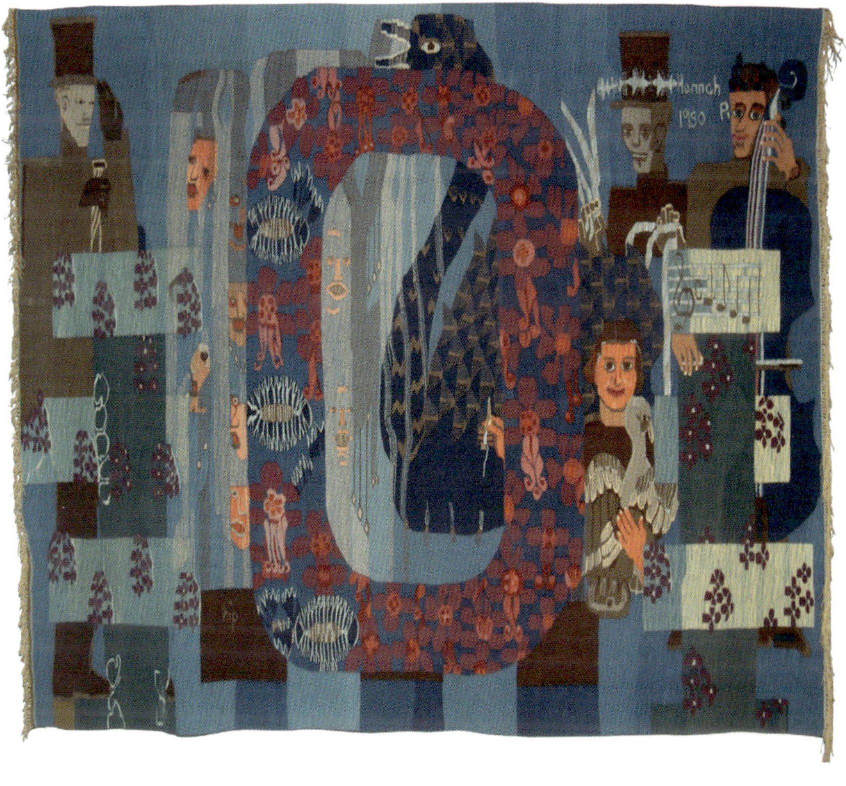
Hennch
1950 R.

"Tapestry art is a fresh breath of air on the art scene. It has not yet exhausted its resources like painting has, wearing the same mask since the Middle Ages."

Diary entry, 25 March 1955

Hannah Ryggen in 1952.

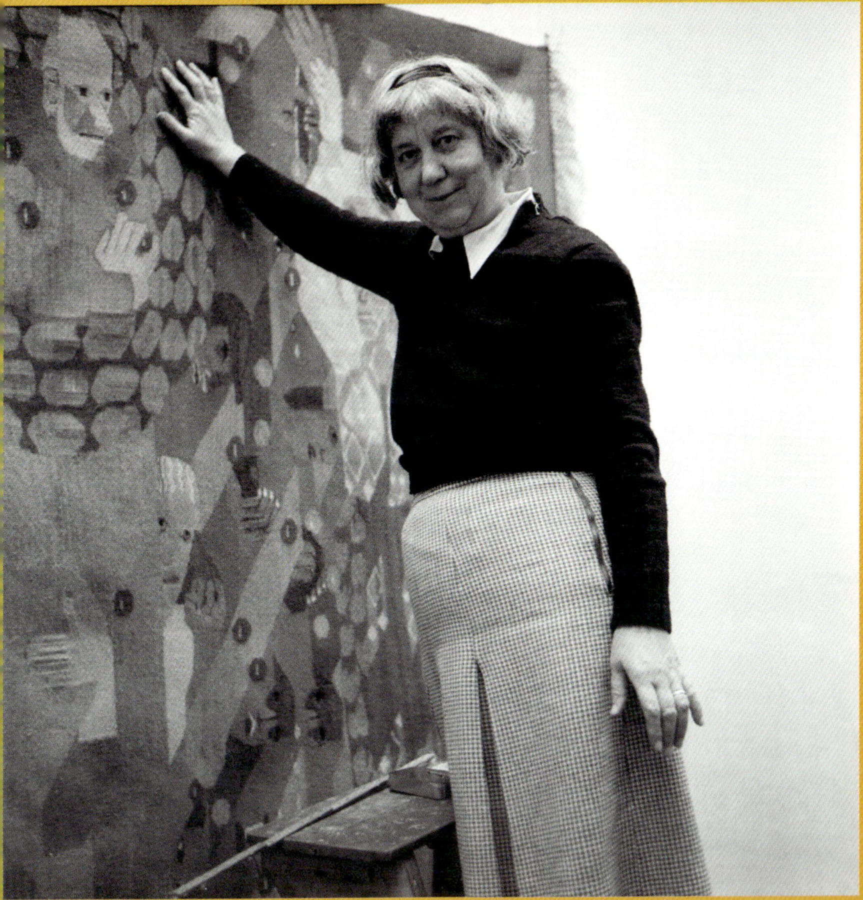

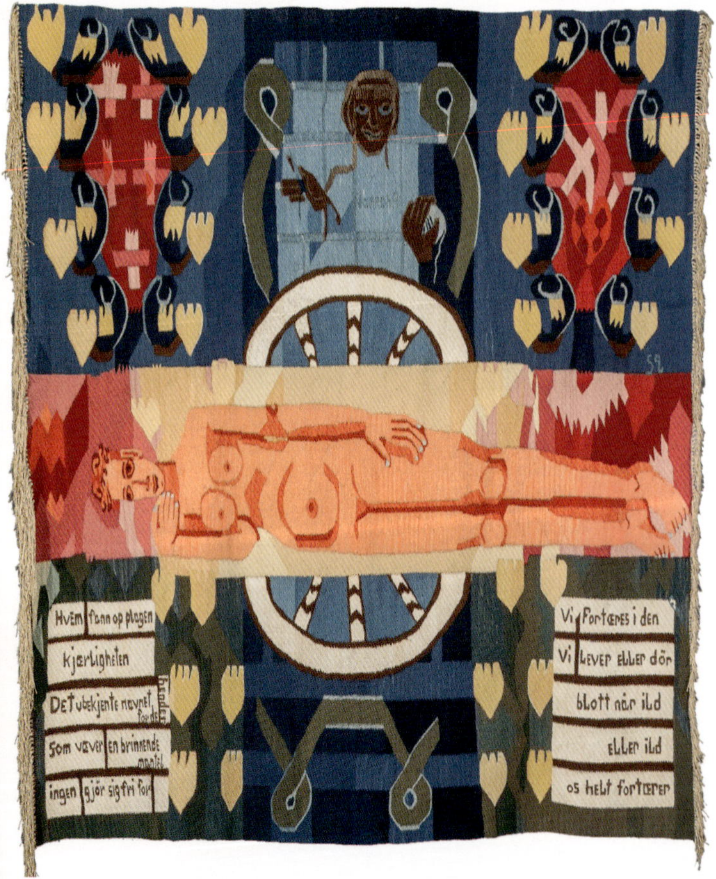

»
Mr. Atom, 1952.
Tapestry in wool and linen.
190 x 170 cm

Poem by T.S. Eliot, 1952.
Tapestry in wool and linen.
180 x 180 cm

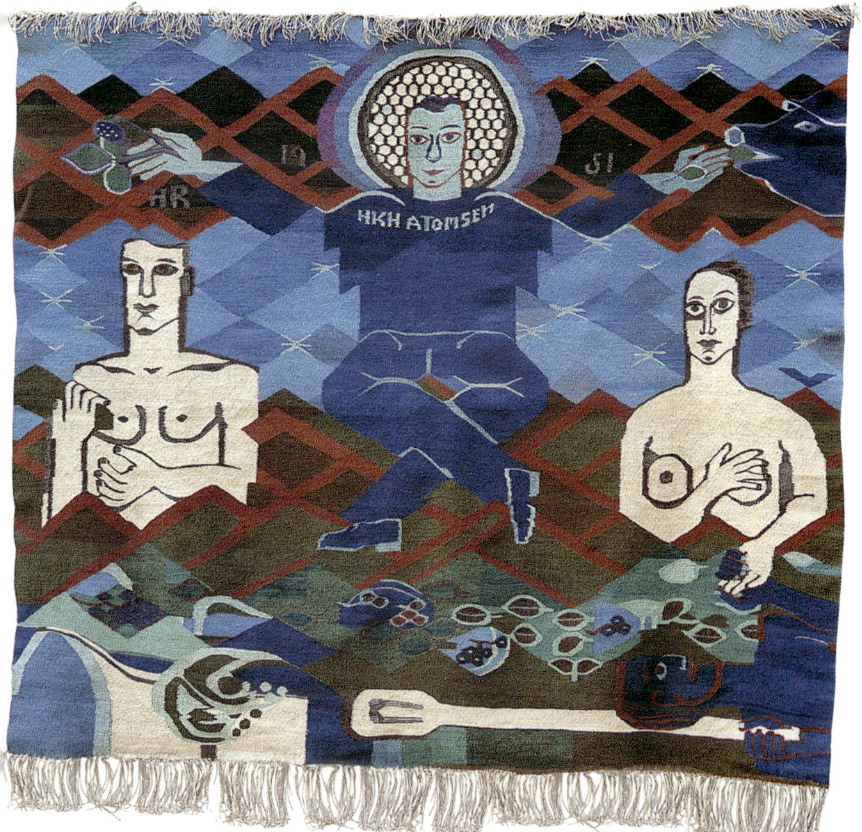

19
51
HR
HKH ATOMSEN

Karsten in Weaver's Heaven, 1953.
Tapestry with pile in wool and linen.
190 x 170 cm

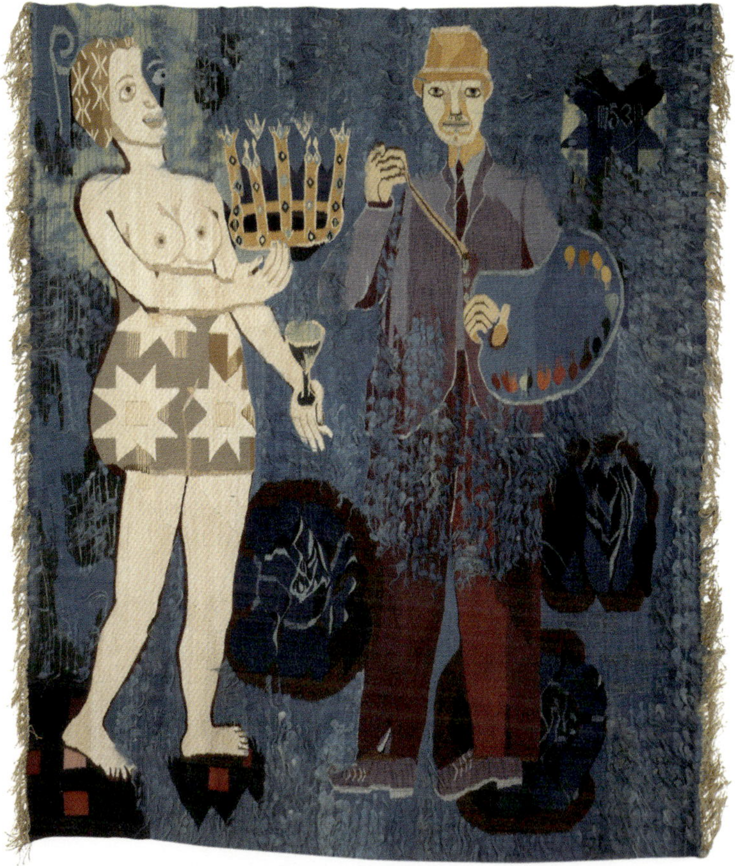

Jul Kvale, 1956.
Tapestry in wool and linen.
190 x 200 cm

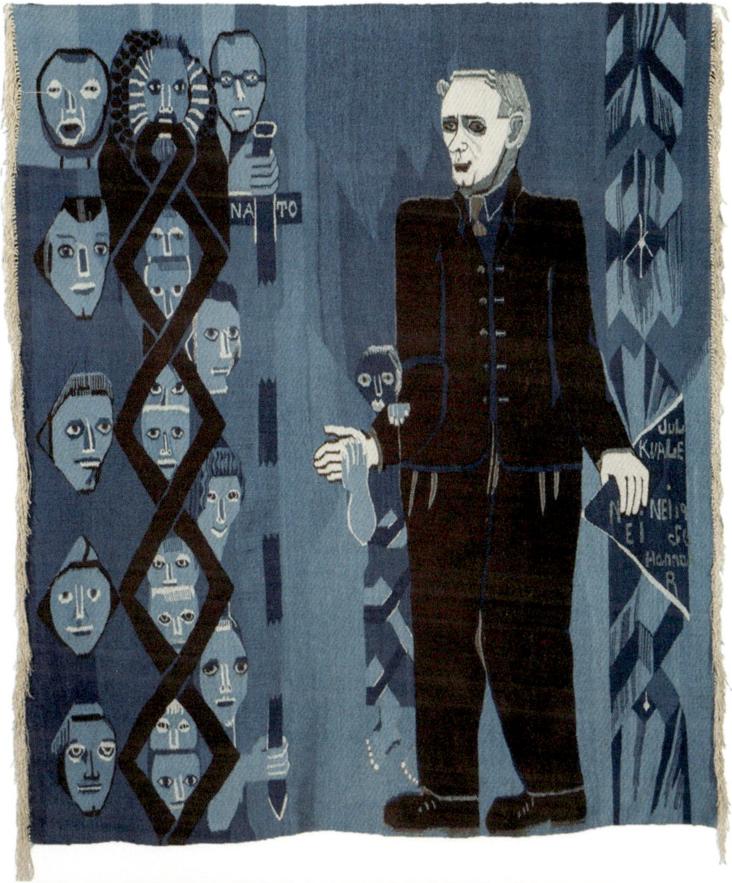
NA TO

"It almost feels like I've cut out and removed a piece of myself."

Upon the completion of We Live upon a Star, *in an interview in* Arbeider-avisa, *23 October 1958*

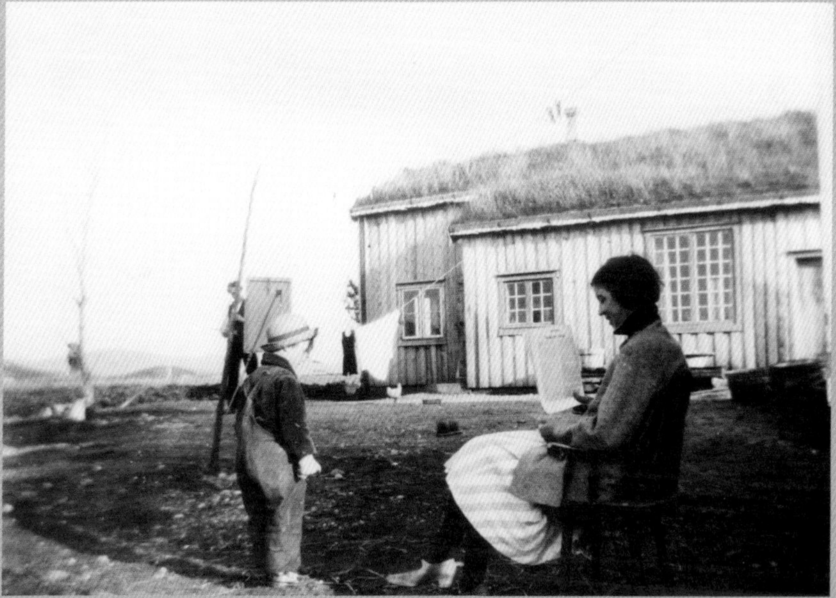

Hannah, Hans and Mona, ca. 1930.

We Live upon a Star, 1958.
Tapestry in wool and linen.
400 x 300 cm

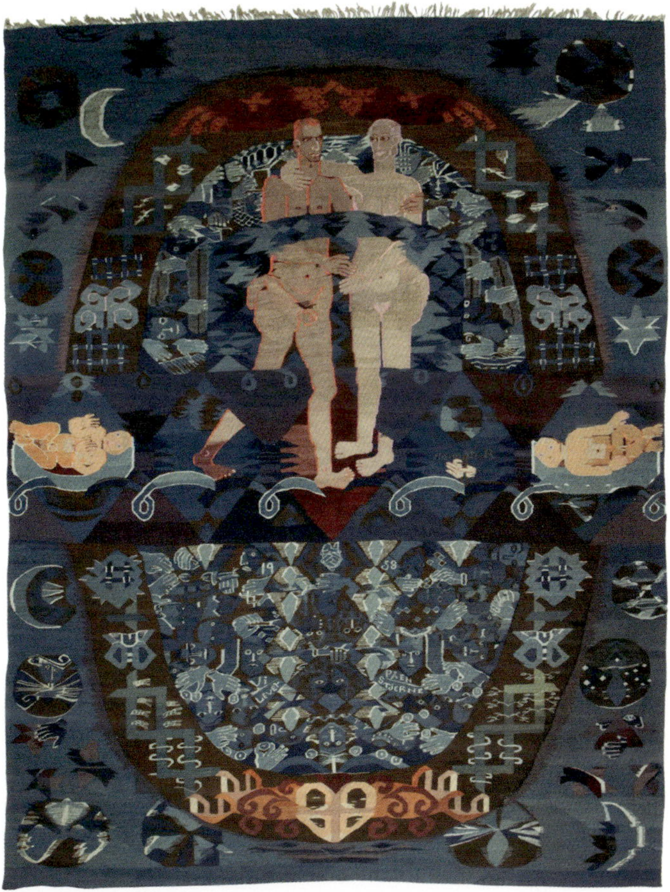

Grey Figure, 1961.
Tapestry in wool and linen.
330 x 235 cm

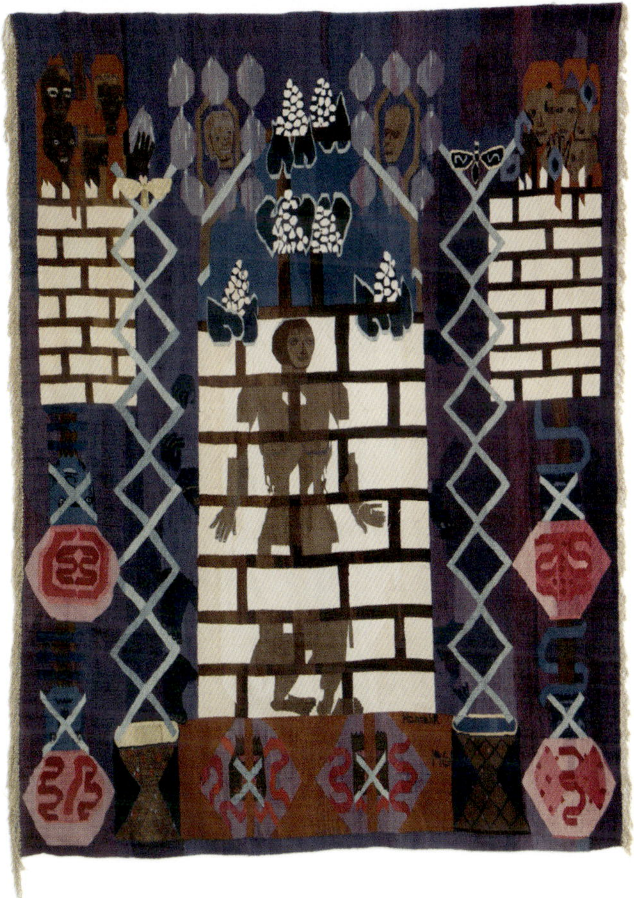

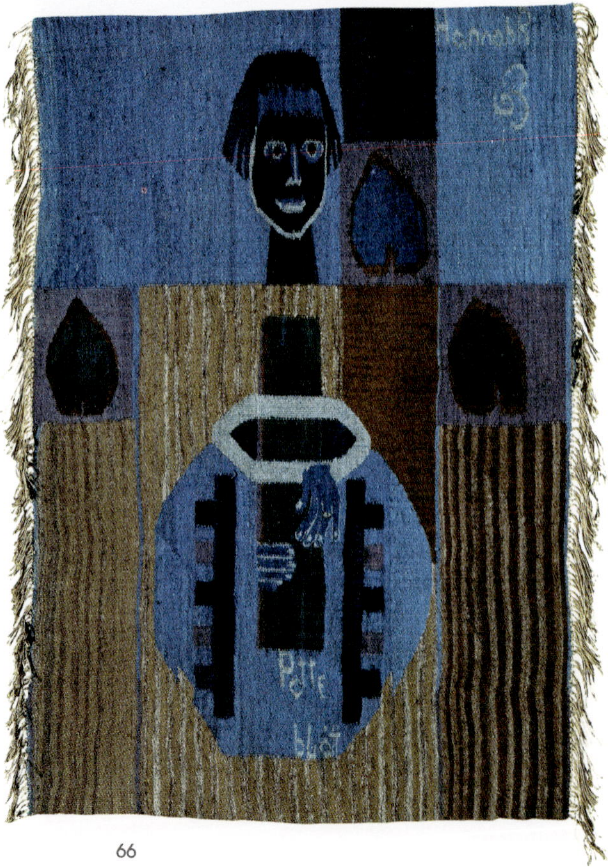

Pot Blue, 1963.
Tapestry in wool
and linen.
120 x 85 cm

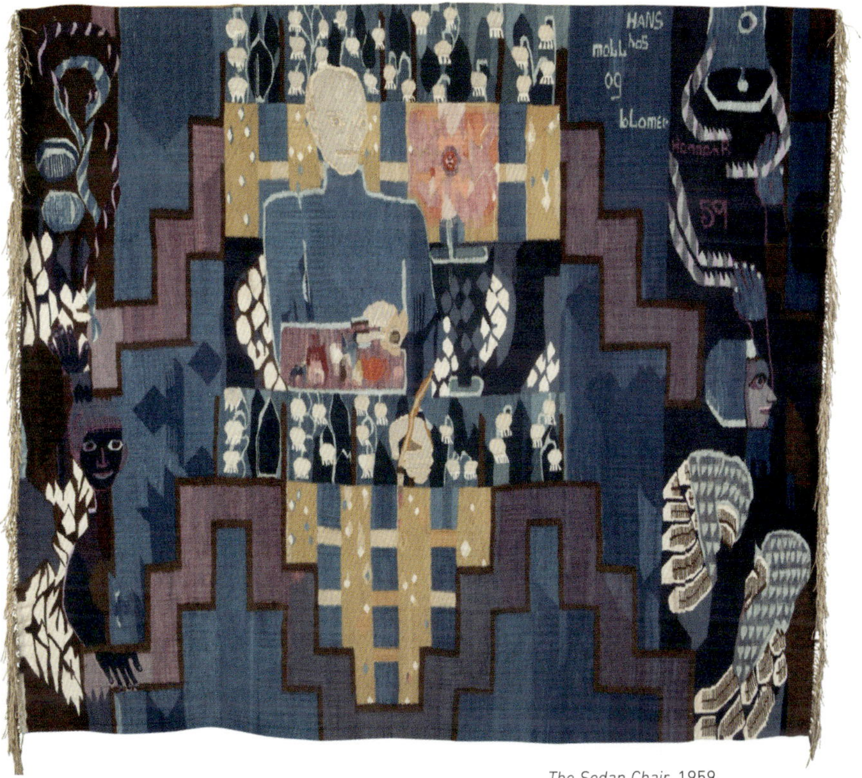

The Sedan Chair, 1959.
Tapestry in wool and linen. 167 x 195 cm

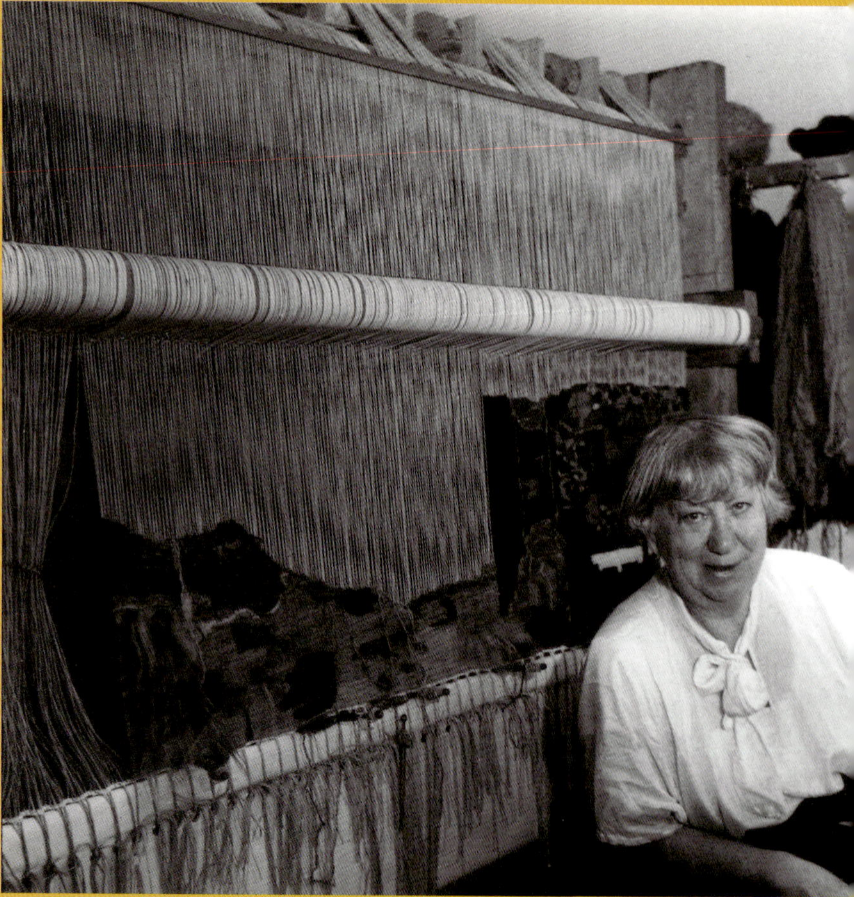

"What do they mean by a 'good' tapestry? I think it should be fantastic, brilliant, alive – the more, the better. But not complete, no – all of my tapestries are merely fragments. They have no beginning or end."

In Albert Steen, Hannah Ryggen - en dikter i veven *(Kunstindustrimuseet, Oslo, 1986), p. 54*

Hannah Ryggen, ca 1960.

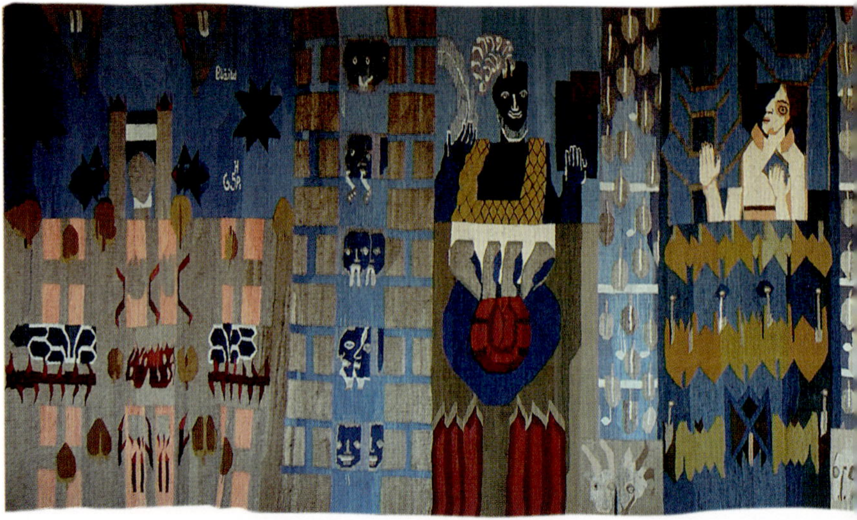

The Troll Wall, 1966.
Tapestry with pile in wool and linen. 190 x 740 cm

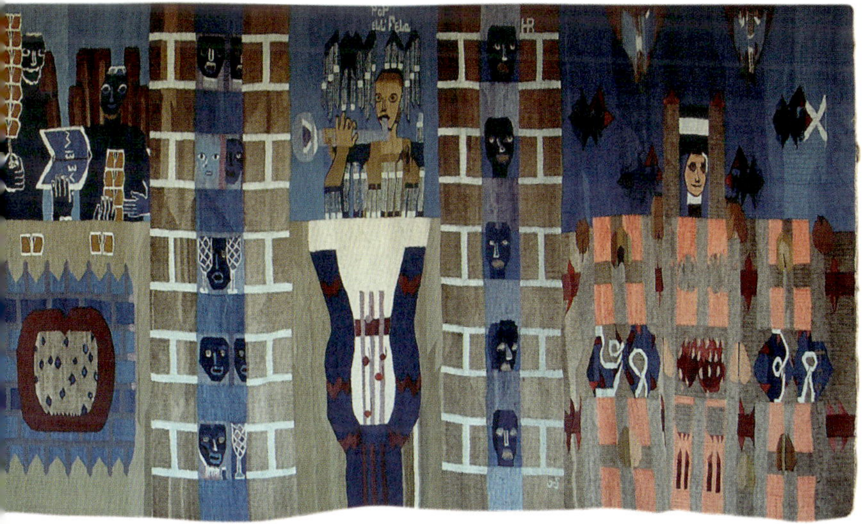

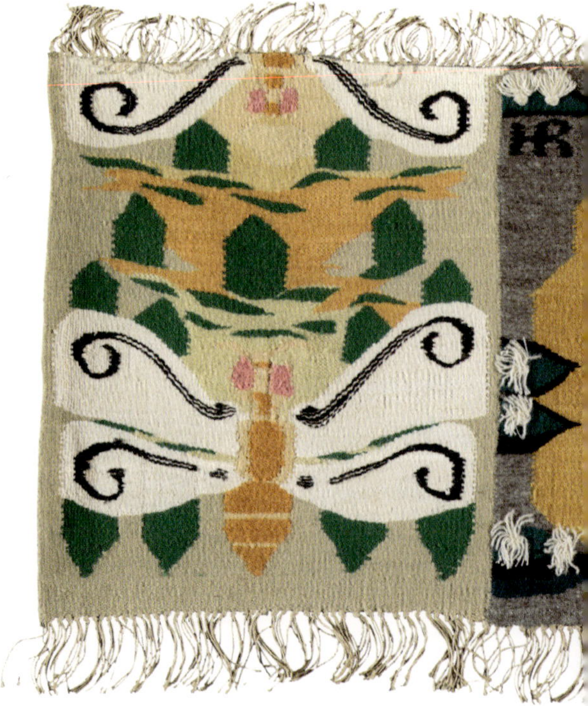

Salvador Dali, 1960–70. Tapestry in wool and linen. 45 x 121 cm

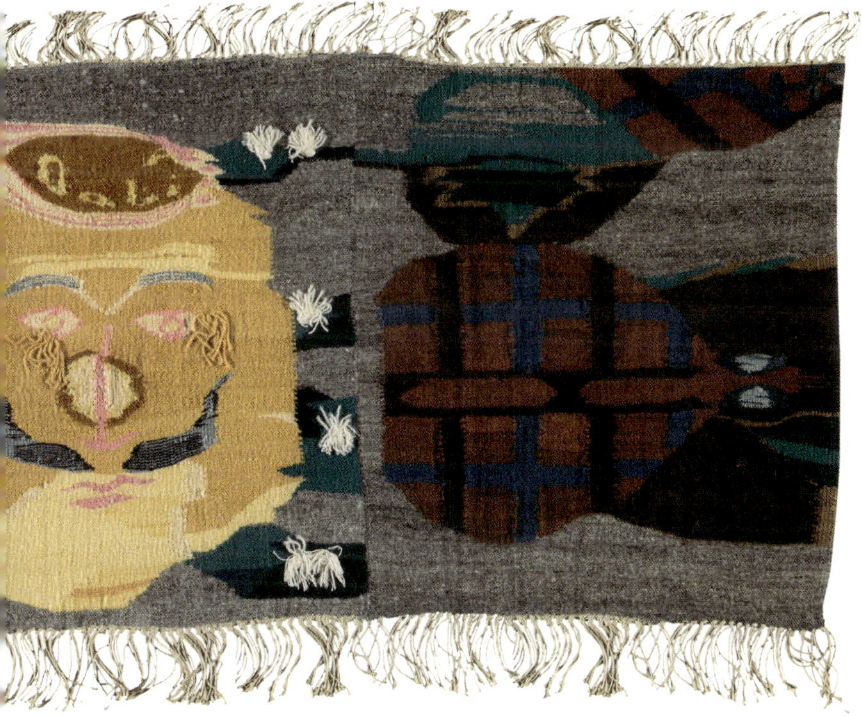

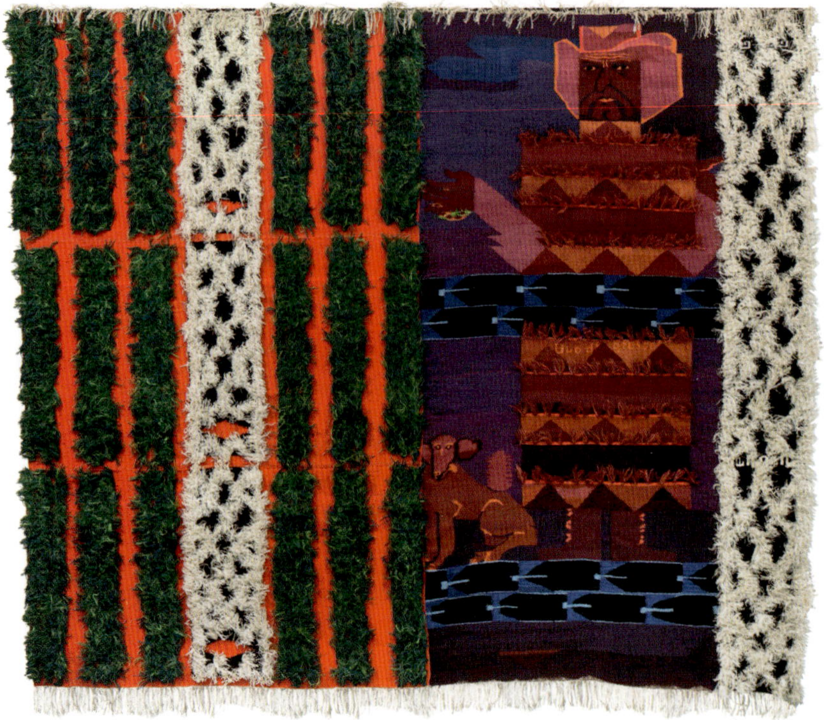

Blood in the Grass, 1966.
Tapestry with pile in wool, linen and rye. 240 x 290 cm

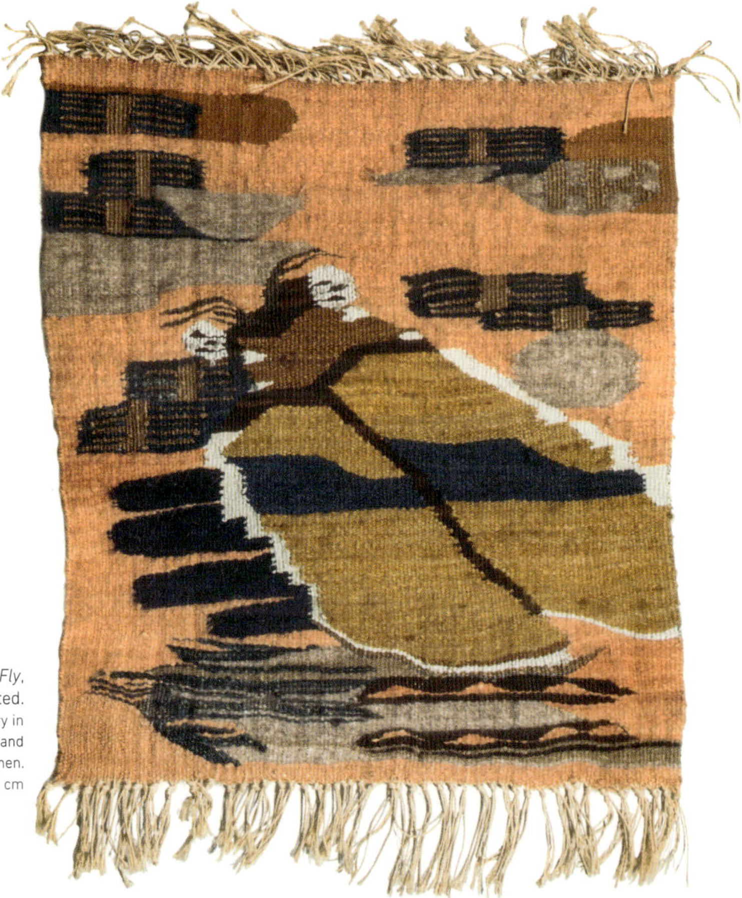

The Fly, undated. Tapestry in wool and linen. 44 x 41.5 cm

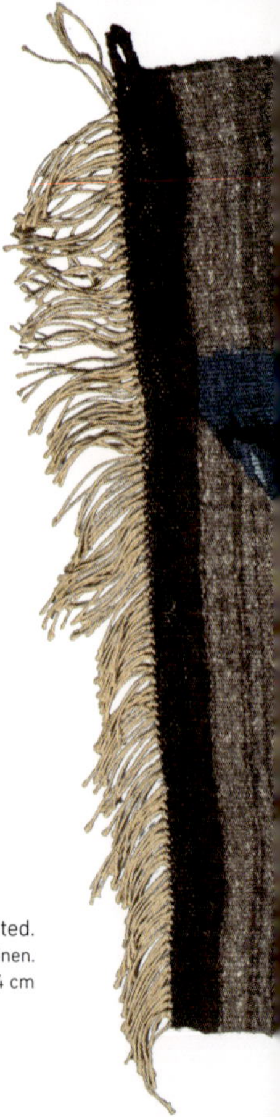

Untitled and undated.
Tapestry in wool and linen.
52.5 x 64 cm

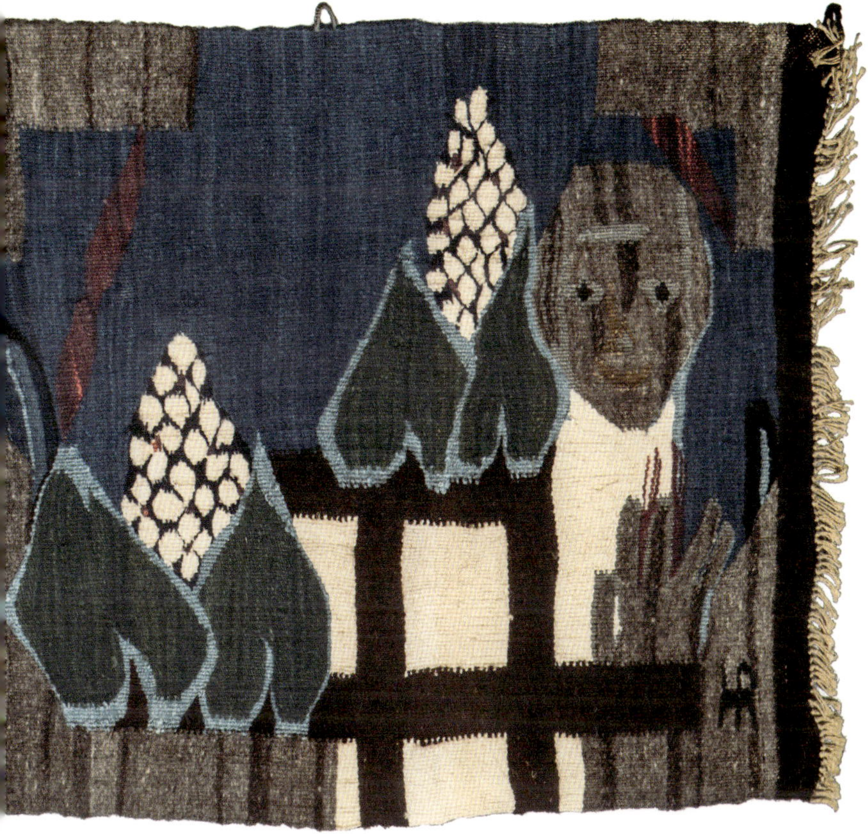

»
Karna and Hannah, 1969.
Tapestry in wool and linen.
176 x 126 cm

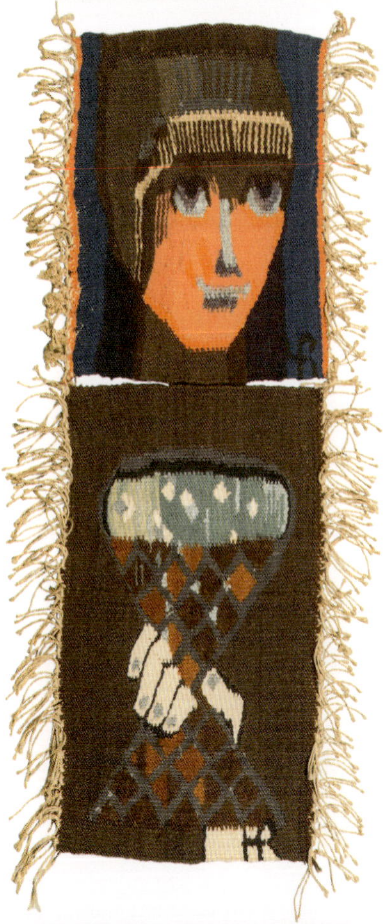

Untitled and undated.
Two smaller pieces put together.
Tapestry in wool and linen.
27 x 20.5 and 35.5 x 21 cm

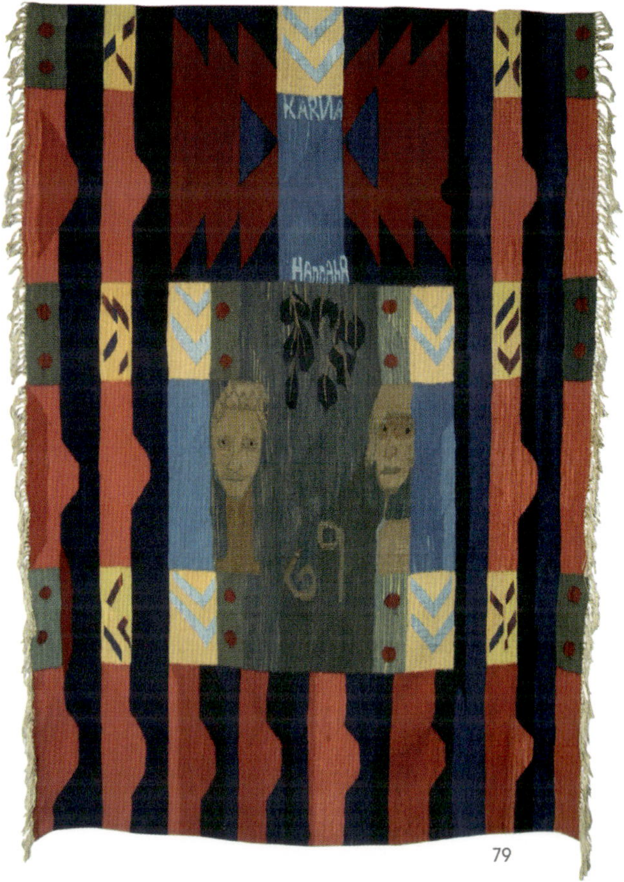

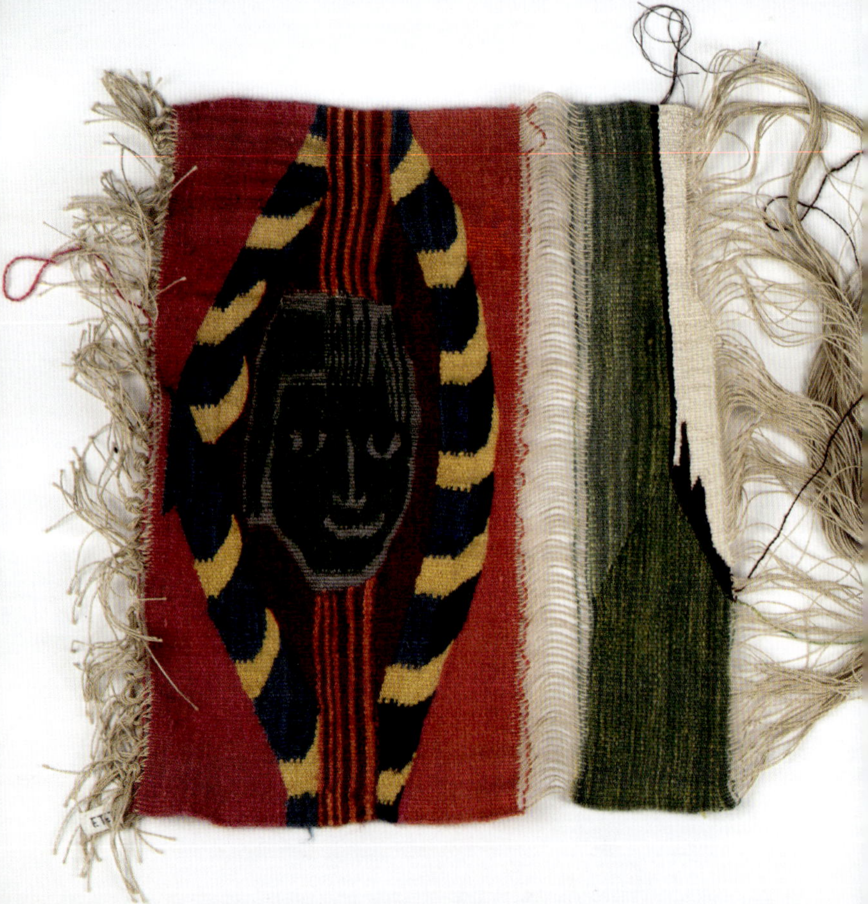

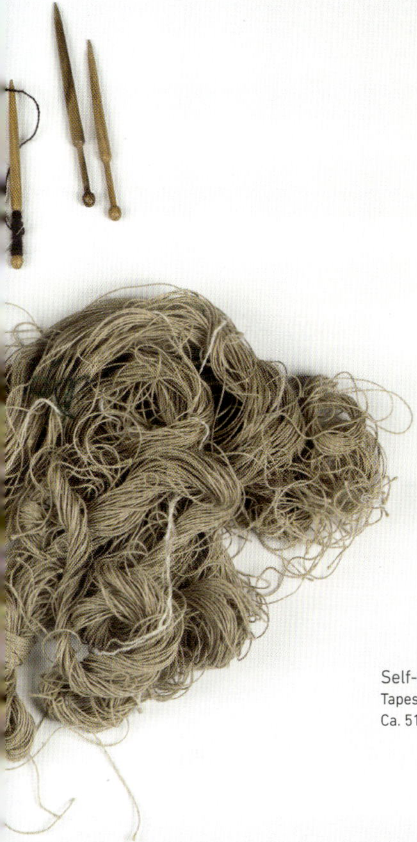

Self-portrait, ca. 1970.
Tapestry in wool and linen.
Ca. 51.5 x 40 cm

"I do everything myself, from scratch. I spin the yarn, dye it, and proceed to weave the threads together, adding my heart to it. That's what makes my weaving art, not just the art of weaving."

Letter to Dyre Vaa, 22 May 1946

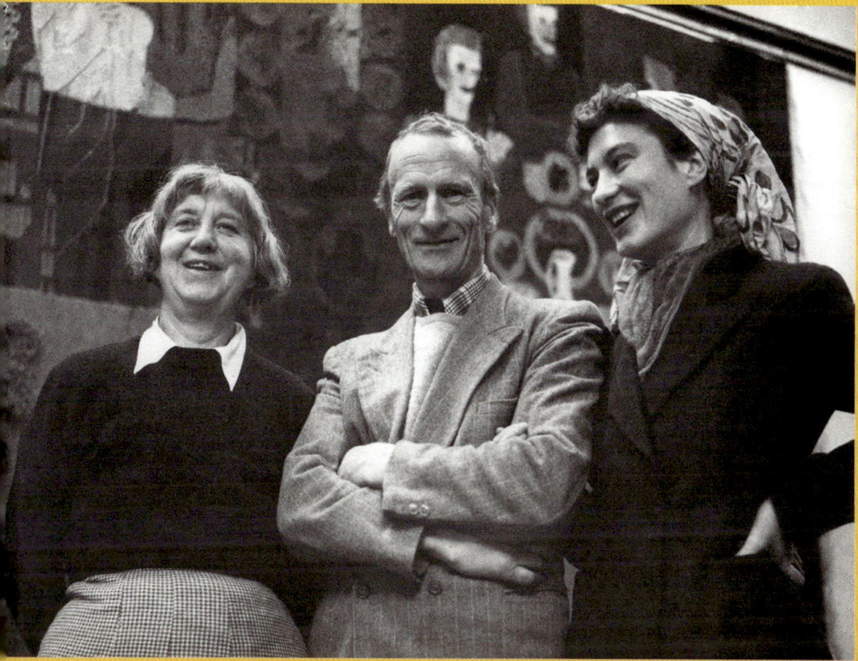

Hannah, Hans and Mona. ca. 1950

The chronology of Hannah Ryggen

1894 Born in Malmö, Sweden, on 21 March as Hanna Josefina Maria Jönsson.

1913-23 Works as a primary school teacher in Malmö. Studies art on the side under the painter Fredrik Krebs in Lund, Sweden.

1914 Sees *The Baltic Exhibition* in Malmö, where avant-garde artists such as Wassily Kandinsky were represented.

1922 Study trip to Dresden, Germany. Meets her future husband, the Norwegian painter Hans Ryggen.

1924 Moves to Ørlandet, Norway. Daughter Mona is born.

1926 Participates in her first exhibition, in Lund, Sweden.

1930 Participates in an anniversary exhibition in Trondheim, Norway.

1933 First major exhibition at the Trondheim Art Association.

1937 Participation in the World Fair in Paris with the tapestry *Etiopia.*

1940 Nordenfjeldske Kunstindustrimuseum acquires their first work.

1944 Husband Hans is arrested by the Nazis. Returns home in 1945.

1946 Travels to Copenhagen, with a major exhibition at the Danish Museum of Art and Design in Copenhagen. Together with her family, goes directly to Bures-Sur-Yvette outside Paris, for a stay of almost 10 months.

1953 Major solo show at Kunstnernes Hus in Oslo. The Museum of Decorative Arts and Design in Oslo acquires their first work.

1954 Exhibition in Petit Palais in Paris.

1955 Receives a comprehensive commission for the new Government Building in Oslo by the architect Erling Viksjø.

1955-56 Major touring exhibition in the U.S.

1956 Death of Hans Ryggen.

1957 Moves from Ørlandet to Trondheim.

1959 Awarded the Prins Eugen gold medal.

1962 Major solo exhibition at the Moderna Museet in Stockholm. Same year has her debut at the National Annual Autumn Exhibition in Oslo, as the first textile artist in the exhibition's history.

1964 Represents Norway at the Venice Biennial.

1965 Nordenfjeldske Kunstindustrimuseum, Trondheim, acquires a large number of works.

1966 Completes a comprehensive commission for the University of Oslo, the monumental *Troll Wall* (*Trollveggen*).

1970 Dies on 2 February in Trondheim, Norway.

Picture register and credits

4 Hannah Ryggen, probably 1920s. Nordenfjeldske Kunstindustrimuseum. Photo: Unknown

16 *Self-portrait*, 1914. Oil on canvas. 40 x 33 cm. Nordenfjeldske Kunstindustrimuseum, Trondheim

18 *The Adulteress* (*Synderinnen*), 1926. Tapestry in wool and linen. 190 x 222 cm. Nordenfjeldske Kunstindustrimuseum, Trondheim. Photo: Anders S. Solberg

19 *Fishing in the Sea of Debt* (*Fiske ved gjeldens hav*), 1933. Tapestry in wool and linen. 145 x 185 cm. Private collection. Photo: Øystein Thorvaldsen/Henie Onstad Kunstsenter

20–21 *We and Our Animals* (*Vi og våre dyr*), 1934. Tapestry in wool and linen. 187.5 x 491 cm. Malmö Museum

22 *First of May Procession* (*Første maitog*), 1935. Rug in wool and linen. 172 x 140 cm. National Museum of Art, Architecture and Design, Oslo

23 *Death of Dreams* (*Drømmedød*), 1936. Tapestry in wool and linen. 235 x 271 cm. Nordenfjeldske Kunstindustrimuseum, Trondheim. Photo: Anders S. Solberg

24–25 *Ethiopia* (*Etiopia*), 1935. Tapestry in wool and linen. 160 x 380 cm. Nordenfjeldske Kunstindustrimuseum, Trondheim. Photo: Anders S. Solberg

26 *Daybreak* (*Morgengry*), 1936. Tapestry in wool and linen.. 297 x 181 cm. National Museum of Art, Architecture and Design, Oslo

27 *Spain* (*La hora se aproxima*), 1938. Tapestry in wool and linen. 193 x 219.5 cm. National Museum of Art, Architecture and Design, Oslo

28–29 *Unmarried Mother* (*Ugift mor*), 1937. Tapestry in wool and linen. 185 x 385 cm. Röhsska Museum. Photo: Christer Hallgren

30 Hannah Jönsson, 1922. Nordenfjeldske Kunstindustrimuseum. Photo: Unknown

32 *Liselotte Hermann decapitated* (*Liselotte Hermann halshuggen*), 1938. Tapestry in wool and linen. 190 x 155 cm. Nordenfjeldske Kunstindustri-

museum, Trondheim. Photo: Anders S. Solberg

33 *Horror* (*Gru*), 1936. Tapestry in wool and linen. 147 x 180 cm. National Museum of Art, Architecture and Design, Oslo

34 *Petter Dass*, 1940. Tapestry with pile in wool and linen, rug. 147 x 258.5 cm. National Museum of Art, Architecture and Design, Oslo

36–37 *6 October 1942*, 1943. Tapestry in wool and linen. 170 x 420 cm. Nordenfjeldske Kunstindustrimuseum, Trondheim. Photo: Anders S. Solberg

39 *Freiheit*, 1941. Tapestry in wool and linen. 190 x 193 cm. Private collection, Oslo. Photo: Jørn Hagen

40 *The Prison Camp Grini* (*Grini*), 1945. Tapestry in wool and linen. 190 x 170 cm. Trondheim Art Museum

41 *Mother's Heart* (*Mors hjerte*), 1947. Tapestry in wool and linen. 195 x 190 cm. Nordenfjeldske Kunstindustrimuseum. Photo: Anders S. Solberg

42 *Schweden*, 1946. Tapestry in wool and linen. 190 x 175 cm. Private collection. Photo: National Museum of Art, Architecture and Design, Oslo

43 *A Free One* (*En fri*), 1948. Tapestry in wool and linen. 190 x 200 cm. Nordenfjeldske Kunstindustrimuseum. Photo: Anders S. Solberg

44 Hannah Ryggen by her loom, date unknown. NTNU University Library. Photo: Unknown

46–47 *The Use of Hands* (*Henders bruk*), 1949. Tapestry in wool and linen. 190 x 210 cm. National Museum of Art, Architecture and Design, Oslo

48–49 *Trojan Horse/The Picasso Tapestry* (*Trojansk hest/Picassoteppet*), 1949–58. Tapestry in wool and linen. 190 x 320 cm. The Norwegian Government. Photo: Kunsthall Oslo

51 *Ja, vi elsker* (the title of the Norwegian national anthem), 1950. Tapestry in wool and linen. 222 x 190 cm. Nordenfjeldske Kunstindustrimuseum, Trondheim

53 Hannah Ryggen in 1952. Photo: Schrøderarchives/Sverresborg

54 *Poem by T.S. Eliot* (*Dikt av T.S. Eliot*), 1952. Tapestry in wool and linen. 180 x 180 cm. Nordenfjeldske Kunstindustrimuseum, Trondheim. Photo: Anders S. Solberg

55 *Mr. Atom* (*Atomsen*), 1952. Tapestry in wool and linen. 190 x 170 cm. Private collection. Photo: National Museum of Art, Architecture and Design, Oslo

57 *Karsten in Weaver's Heaven* (*Karsten i vevhimmelen*), 1953. Tapestry with pile in wool and linen. 190 x 170 cm. Nationalmuseum, Stockholm

59 *Jul Kvale*, 1956. Tapestry in wool and linen. 190 x 200 cm. Nordenfjeldske Kunstindustrimuseum. Photo: Anders S. Solberg

61 Hannah, Hans and Mona, ca. 1930. NTNU University Library. Photo: Unknown

63 *We Live upon a Star* (*Vi lever på en stjerne*), 1958. Tapestry in wool and linen. 400 x 300 cm. Statsbygg. Photo: Bevaringstjenestene Museumssenteret i Hordaland

65 *Grey Figure* (*Grå figur*), 1961. Tapestry in wool and linen. 330 x 235 cm. Nordenfjeldske Kunstindustrimuseum, Trondheim. Photo: Kirsti Hovde

66 *Pot Blue* (*Potteblått*), 1963. Tapestry in wool and linen. 120 x 85 cm. National Museum of Art, Architecture and Design, Oslo

67 *The Sedan Chair* (*Bærestolen*), 1959. Tapestry in wool and linen. 167 x 195 cm. Stockholms Stadsmuseum

68 Hannah Ryggen, ca. 1960. Photo: Unknown

70–71 *The Troll Wall* (*Trollveggen*), 1966. Tapestry with pile in wool and linen. 190 x 740 cm. University of Oslo. Photo: Ståle Skogstad

72–73 *Salvador Dali*, 1960–70. Tapestry in wool and linen. 45 x 121 cm. National Museum of Art, Architecture and Design, Oslo

74 *Blood in the Grass* (*Blod i gresset*), 1966. Tapestry with pile in wool, linen and rye. 240 x 290 cm. KODE Art Museums and Composer Homes, Bergen

75 *The Fly* (*Flugan*), undated. Tapestry in wool and linen. 44 x 41.5 cm. Nordenfjeldske Kunstindustri-museum, Trondheim. Photo: Anders S. Solberg

76 Untitled, undated. Tapestry in wool and linen. 52.5 x 64 cm. Nordenfjeldske Kunstindustrimuseum, Trondheim. Photo: Anders S. Solberg

77 Untitled, undated. Two smaller pieces put together. Tapestry in wool and linen. 27 x 20.5 and 35.5 x 21 cm. Nordenfjeldske Kunstindustri-museum, Trondheim. Photo: Anders S. Solberg

78 *Karna and Hannah*, 1969. Tapestry in wool and linen. 176 x 126 cm. Nordenfjeldske Kunstindustri-museum, Trondheim. Photo: Jette C. Petersen

80–81 Self-portrait, ca. 1970. Tapestry in wool and linen. Ca. 51.5 x 40 cm. Nordenfjeldske Kunstindustrimuseum, Trondheim. Photo: Uta Freia Beer

83 Hannah, Hans and Mona. ca. 1950. Photo: Unknown

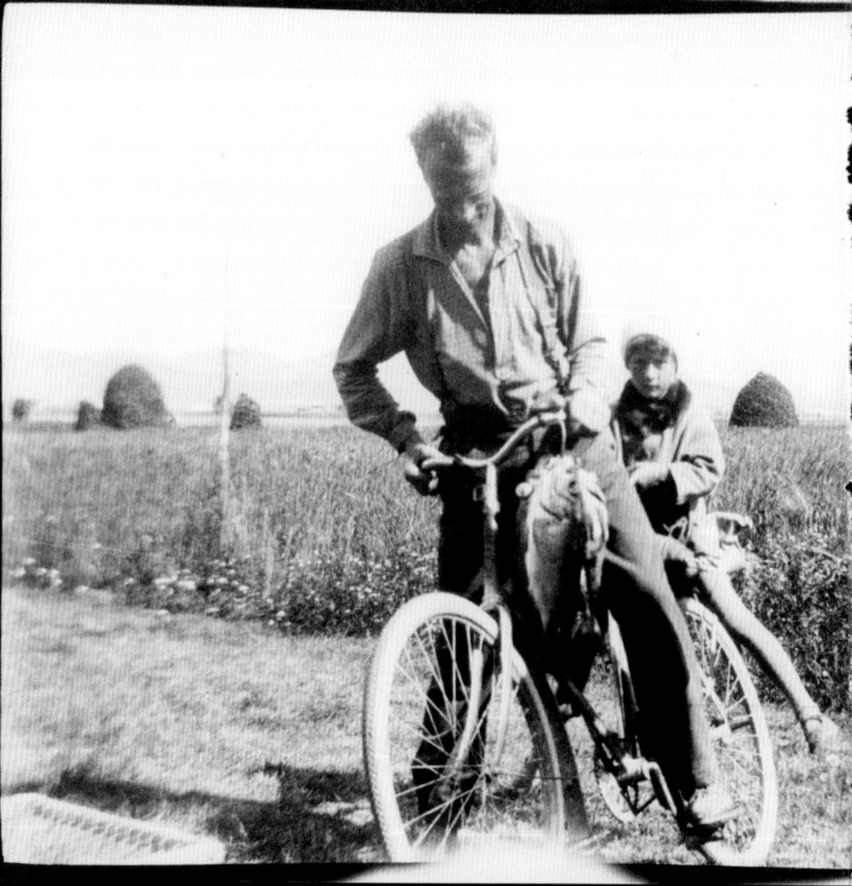